BOY BANDS

ULTIMATE TRIVIA BOOK

BOY BANDS

ULTIMATE TRIVIA BOOK

Test Your Superfan Status and Relive the Most Iconic Boy Band Moments

Karah-Leigh Hancock

EPIC INK

This book is dedicated to the boy band fangirls of the world. We are a special breed of fan. We are protective of our boys. We are fierce when it comes to promoting and supporting our favorite groups. God forbid someone says something bad about them.

Whether it's the fangirls who sat and watched the Beatles on *The Ed Sullivan Show* or the fangirls who hope that one day One Direction will get back together like the Jonas Brothers, I salute you.

Keep fighting the good fight.

Contents

INTRODUCTION

What's the deal with boy bands?

According to *Merriam-Webster's Dictionary*, a boy band is "a small ensemble of males in their teens or twenties who play pop songs geared especially to a young female audience." Boy bands, love 'em or hate 'em (though, let's be honest, what's not to love?), have been a constant presence in the music scene since long before the Beatles, since the days of street corner singers and barbershop quartets. From Dion and the Belmonts sweetly singing "In the Still of the Night" or "A Teenager In Love" to the Penguins belting out their only hit, "Earth Angel," vocal harmony groups have always been around—and making teenagers swoon.

Boy bands, in all their many iterations, are mesmerizing. Some fit the mold perfectly and immediately come to mind when you bring up the topic, bands like New Kids on the Block, Backstreet Boys, and One Direction. And there are some—from the Beatles to the Bay City Rollers to the fourteen-member South Korean group, Seventeen (admittedly more than just a "small ensemble")—that may seem outside the scope at first glance. But boy bands come in all shapes and sizes, and whether you prefer the smooth moves of K-pop groups or five harmonizing hunks from the States, there's a boy band for every flavor of fan out there.

But what is it about boy bands that we find so fascinating? Is it the synchronized dance moves? It can't be, because not all boy bands can pull that off—though we certainly appreciate the ones that can! Is it their guitar solos? No, because not all boy bands play instruments.

Is it the harmonies? Absolutely.

Boy bands, like the groups in the golden age of music, are known for sweet voices that blend perfectly together, like a magical music potion. Their music not only brings joy but also has a unique ability to make people feel like they're part of something bigger, a global community of dedicated fans who share their love for these groups.

If heaven had a soundtrack, it would sound like the chorus of a boy band song.

How to Use This Book

If you could call into *TRL* to vote for "All I Have to Give" against "I Drive Myself Crazy," you should be able to use this book easily. If you've tested the trendy waters of boy band fandoms and survived, then you can get through anything!

The book is broken into three sections by decades. Each section features a number of "main" quizzes, with twenty-five questions each, and then a short bonus quiz about a different band, with five questions. Please note that if it were up to us, every band would get hundreds of questions and this book would be a thousand pages long! As it is, we're working with the space we've got, but we've still crammed in as many of your favorite bands, songs, albums, and group members as we could think of.

Answer each multiple choice or true/false question to the best of your ability. (We know you probably already know the answers, especially about your favorite bands!) Check your answers against the answer key after each quiz to see if you're right. Then find out how you rank as a know-it-all for your favorite boy band!

Rating System

As mentioned on the How to Use This Book page, all the main boy band quizzes have twenty-five questions each, and the bonus quizzes have five questions each. You get one point for every right answer in the main quiz and two points for each bonus question you get right. Why two points? Typically, these boy bands are not as big as their counterparts and sometimes are not as well known. The more you know about these, the bigger boy band fan you are!

SUPER FAN
You are a huge fan of this band, and it *shows.*

BOY BAND FAN
You definitely know the groups and some of their history.

CASUAL FAN
You know the songs and maybe a few facts —keep trying!

IMPOSTER
You may know one or two songs. You have your work cut out for you.

Are you their BIGGEST FAN?

Once you've taken all the quizzes in this book, take a look at the point ranges below to see where you land on the fan scale.

100–199
POINTS

BOY BAND FAN-IN-TRAINING

You know enough boy band facts to get by and that makes you a fan.

200–325
POINTS

BOY BAND GROUPIE

You've seen a lot of boy band concerts and know them very well.

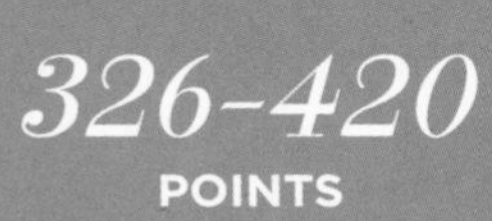

326–420 POINTS

BOY BAND EXPERT

You know a great deal about boy bands, more so than the standard boy band fan.

421+ POINTS

PROFESSIONAL BOY BAND CONNOISSEUR

You know boy bands inside and out. Are you sure you don't have a degree in the subject?

Scoring Sheet

THE 1960S AND 1970S

QUIZ #1: The Beatles __ / 25

Bonus #1: The Monkees __ / 10

QUIZ #2: Jackson 5 __ / 25

Bonus #2: The Osmonds __ / 10

Total: __ / 70

THE 1980S AND 1990S

QUIZ #1: New Edition __ / 25

Bonus #1: Menudo __ / 10

QUIZ #2: New Kids on the Block __ / 25

Bonus #2: Color Me Badd __ / 10

QUIZ #3: Boyz II Men __ / 25

Bonus #3: All-4-One __ / 10

QUIZ #4: Take That __ / 25

Bonus #4: Boyzone __ / 10

QUIZ #5: Backstreet Boys __ / 25

Bonus #5: Westlife __ / 10

QUIZ #6: NSYNC __ / 25

Bonus #6: 5ive __ / 10

QUIZ #7: 98 Degrees __ / 25

Bonus #7: 3Deep __ / 10

QUIZ #8: Hanson __ / 25

Bonus #8: BBMak __ / 10

QUIZ #9: B2K __ / 25

Bonus #9: soulDecision __ / 10

Total: __ / 315

THE 2000S AND 2010S

QUIZ #1: O-Town __ / 25

Bonus #1: 2Gether __ / 10

QUIZ #2: Jonas Brothers __ / 25

Bonus #2: Dream Street __ / 10

QUIZ #3: Big Time Rush __ / 25

Bonus #3: CNCO __ / 10

QUIZ #4: One Direction __ / 25

Bonus #4: The Wanted __ / 10

QUIZ #5: BTS __ / 25

Bonus #5: Tomorrow x Together __ / 10

Total: __ / 175

Grand Total: __ / 560

1960s & 1970s

1960s & 1970s

The Beatles

In a world that was fixated on Elvis Presley, his love songs, and his dance moves, we were given the gift of the Beatles. The Beatles are sometimes called the original boy band. Sure, they played their own instruments and wrote their own songs, but they didn't dance. As you will find out in later chapters, it was really only the boy bands of the 1980s, 1990s, and early 2000s that did the synchronized dance moves.

But the Beatles were the first group to cause pandemonium among teenage girls and to cause grown women to throw themselves at buses, cars, and sometimes the band members themselves. When you hear about girls stowing away on the Backstreet Boys' tour buses? It happened to the Beatles first. John, Ringo, Paul, and George were the first group that had their pictures plastered on teenage girls' walls.

To many, the Beatles were more than just a band—they were artists. While Van Gogh painted with paintbrushes, John and Paul created art with their words and melodies as two of the greatest songwriters to ever live.

1960s & 1970s

The Beatles

1. What was the name of John Lennon's first band?

A. The British Lads

B. The Beetles

C. The Quarrymen

D. The Braves

2. What band did Ringo leave to join the Beatles?

A. Rory Storm and the Hurricanes

B. Captain Geetch and the Shrimp Shack Shooters

C. The Bobby Pins

D. Tornados and Hurricanes

3. John Lennon studied what subject while attending Liverpool College?

A. Biology

B. Music

C. Art

D. History

4. Who was John Lennon's hero?

A. Frank Sinatra

B. Elvis Presley

C. Buddy Holly

D. Chuck Berry

5. What was the name of the Beatles' first single?

A. "Can't Buy Me Love"

B. "I Wanna Hold Your Hand"

C. "Twist and Shout"

D. "Love Me Do"

6. Who was the Beatles' manager?

A. Brian Epstein

B. Ed Epstein

C. Brian Windsor

D. Ed White

7. What was the name of the Beatles' first album?

A. *Love Me Do*

B. *Please, Please Me*

C. *Can't Buy Me Love*

D. *People and Places*

8. The Beatles didn't want to visit America until what had occurred?

A. They had a #1 record.

B. Elvis went into the army.

C. They sold a million albums.

D. They released two singles.

9. Who was the first Beatle to get married?

A. Paul

B. John

C. Ringo

D. George

10. Where was the first Beatles concert in the United States?

A. Yankee Stadium

B. Washington Coliseum

C. Carnegie Hall

D. Atlanta-Fulton County Stadium

11. When did the Beatles first arrive in New York City?

A. January 4, 1964

B. February 1, 1965

C. February 7, 1964

D. March 9, 1963

12. What was the term that was coined after so many British groups became popular in the United States?

A. The British Invasion

B. The Queen's Lads

C. Teatime

D. The Knights' Renegade

13. Which Beatle is crossing Abbey Road first on the famous album cover?

A. Paul

B. John

C. George

D. Ringo

14. Who was "Hey Jude" written for?

A. George's daughter, Judith

B. Ringo's cat, Jude

C. John's son, Julian

D. Paul's mom, June

15. Who was the first Beatle to release a solo song?

A. Paul

B. George

C. Ringo

D. John

16. Who was *not* featured on the cover of *Sgt. Pepper's Lonely Hearts Club Band*?

A. Marilyn Monroe

B. Edgar Allan Poe

C. Shirley Temple

D. Queen Elizabeth

17. What was the name of the Beatles' last movie?

A. *A Day in the Life*

B. *Magical Mystery Tour*

C. *Strawberry Fields*

D. *Let It Be*

18. While recording The Beatles, better known as the White Album, who quit the band for three weeks, leaving the group as a trio to record songs such as "Back in the U.S.S.R."?

A. Ringo

B. Paul

C. John

D. George

19. Which Beatle actually grew up near a place named Strawberry Field?

A. George

B. Paul

C. John

D. Ringo

20. In which city did the Beatles perform their last concert?

A. London

B. Mexico City

C. San Francisco

D. Boston

21. What 1979 movie directed by Robert Zemeckis and coproduced by Steven Spielberg is about a group of New Jersey teenagers going to New York to see the Beatles' first television appearance?

A. *Help!*

B. *I Wanna Hold Your Hand*

C. *A Hard Day's Night*

D. *A Day in the Life*

22. What day in January has been known as World Beatles Day since 2001?

A. January 1

B. June 20

C. January 16

D. June 25

23. In 1985, which singer purchased Associated Television (ATV) for $47.5 million, which also gave him control of more than two hundred songs by the Beatles?

A. Michael Jackson

B. David Bowie

C. Willie Nelson

D. Frank Sinatra

24. How many Grammys did the Beatles win?

A. Four

B. None

C. Seven

D. Ten

25. True or False: *The Ed Sullivan Show* was *not* the Beatles' American television debut.

Answers: 1. C; 2. A; 3. C; 4. B; 5. D; 6. A; 7. B; 8. A; 9. B; 10. B; 11. C; 12. A; 13. B; 14. C; 15. B; 16. D; 17. D; 18. A; 19. C; 20. C; 21. B; 22. D; 23. A; 24. C; 25. True: They appeared on a TV show called *Huntley-Brinkley Report* a few months before.

BONUS
THE MONKEES

The Monkees are an American band that was formed in 1966 for a television show after two producers were inspired by the Beatles' *A Hard Day's Night* and *Help!* Much like the Beatles, the group started out with mop-top hairstyles, portraying a band similar to the Fab Four for a television show. Much like boy bands of the '90s, the Monkees were manufactured for one reason—to entertain and drive girls crazy with their television show. But eventually the Monkees became a band of their own.

1. What was the name of the Monkees' first single?

A. "Daydream Believer"
B. "Last Train to Clarksville"
C. "Valleri"
D. "What Am I Doing Hangin' Around?"

2. When was The Monkees television show canceled?

A. February 1968
B. July 1973
C. May 1970
D. March 1968

3. Which two members of the group appeared in all fifty-eight episodes of the show?

A. Peter Tork and Davy Jones

B. Micky Dolenz and Davy Jones

C. Peter Tork and Micky Dolenz

D. Michael Nesmith and Peter Tork

4. Which TV character was the president of the local Davy Jones fan club and believed she could get him to perform at her school prom?

A. Marcia Brady *(The Brady Bunch)*

B. Laurie Partridge *(The Partridge Family)*

C. Penny Woods *(Good Times)*

D. Jan Brady *(The Brady Bunch)*

5. True or False: The Monkees outsold the Beatles and the Rolling Stones in 1967.

Answers: 1. B; 2. D; 3. C; 4. A; 5. True

75

1960s & 1970s

Jackson 5

Known as the "First Family of Soul," the Jackson 5 was one of the first pop vocal groups that consisted solely of brothers. The Jacksons, unlike other groups of the time, pushed barriers and became one of the first African American crossover acts to create a following.

The group performed for the first time in 1964 when the youngest member of the group, Michael, was just six years old. Two years later, the brothers won a talent show in their hometown and began their path to stardom. They are said to have laid the groundwork for teen pop music, selling more than 100 million albums worldwide. And as we all know, Michael went on to become the King of Pop.

1960s & 1970s

Jackson 5

1. What is the Jackson 5's hometown?

A. Gary, Indiana

B. Columbus, Ohio

C. Jacksonville, Florida

D. Jackson, Mississippi

2. Who is not a founding member of the Jackson 5?

A. Michael

B. Jackie

C. Tito

D. Randy

3. Where did the brothers rehearse before they began performing professionally?

A. Their garage

B. The sidewalk

C. Their living room

D. Their school auditorium

4. **Which singer sent the Jackson 5's demo to Motown Records after seeing them win a talent competition at the Apollo Theatre?**

A. Aretha Franklin

B. Diana Ross

C. Gladys Knight

D. Dionne Warrick

5. **What was the name of the Jackson 5's first single?**

A. "I'll Be There"

B. "I Want You Back"

C. "A-B-C"

D. "Who's Lovin' You"

6. **How many No. 1 hits did the Jackson 5 have?**

A. 5

B. 3

C. 4

D. 10

7. **Which song did the Jackson 5 sing during their first talent show in 1966 to win the top prize?**

A. "My Girl"

B. "Superstar"

C. "Tutti Fruitti"

D. "I Want to Hold Your Hand"

8. Which singer did the Jackson 5 open for and impress enough for them to send the brothers to Detroit to record an audition with Motown?

A. Diana Ross

B. Otis Williams

C. Bobby Taylor

D. Gladys Horton

9. **True or False:** The Jackson brothers voiced their own characters in their Jackson 5ive Saturday morning cartoon series.

10. **Which Jackson 5 sibling began acting on the group's 1976 variety show at the age of ten?**

A. Rebbie
B. Randy
C. Latoya
D. Janet

11. **Who was the first member to leave the Jackson 5?**

A. Michael
B. Tito
C. Jermaine
D. Marlon

12. **True or False:** The Jackson 5 won six Grammy Awards.

13. **Which "Golden Girl" was a guest on the group's 1977 variety show, *The Jacksons*?**

A. Bea Arthur
B. Rue McClanahan
C. Betty White
D. Estelle Getty

14. Janet Jackson starred on what '70s sitcom as a character named Penny?

A. *Good Times*

B. *Three's Company*

C. *The Partridge Family*

D. *Maude*

15. Motown launched Michael Jackson's solo career in what year?

A. 1983

B. 1972

C. 1978

D. 1985

16. When the Jackson 5 decided to leave Motown Records, what could they not take with them?

A. Their music

B. Michael

C. Their name

D. Their outfits

17. On the set of which movie did Michael Jackson meet Quincy Jones, who would go on to produce three of his biggest solo albums?

A. *The Wiz*

B. *This Place Hotel*

C. *State of Shock*

D. *Home Alone*

18. Which soda company were the brothers filming a commercial for when Michael's hair caught on fire?

A. Pepsi

B. Coca-Cola

C. Mountain Dew

D. Dr Pepper

19. When the group left Motown Records for Epic Records, which brother stayed behind and was replaced by youngest brother Randy?

A. Michael

B. Jermaine

C. Tito

D. Marlon

20. Michael Jackson cowrote the charity single "We Are the World" with which singer?

A. Mick Jagger

B. Paul McCartney

C. George Michael

D. Lionel Richie

21. To whom did Michael dedicate his record-breaking album, *Thriller*?

A. Madonna

B. His mother, Katherine

C. Bubbles the monkey

D. His sister, Latoya

22. Marlon Jackson left the music business in 1989 and did what?

A. Became a lawyer

B. Opened a car lot

C. Went into real estate

D. Opened a theme park

23. What was the name of the legendary TV miniseries about the Jackson family?

A. *The Jacksons: An American Dream*

B. *Legacy: The Jacksons*

C. *2300 Jackson Street*

D. *American Dream*

24. Which Jackson brother is also the father of the '90s boy band 3T?

A. Jermaine

B. Tito

C. Randy

D. Michael

25. True or False: The Rock and Roll Hall of Fame inducted the Jackson 5 in 1997.

Answers: 1. A; 2. D; 3. C; 4. C (Unfortunately, the band was rejected); 5. B; 6. C; 7. A; 8. C; 9. False; 10. D; 11. C; 12. False; 13. C; 14. A; 15. B; 16. C; 17. A; 18. A; 19. B; 20. D; 21. B; 22. C; 23. A; 24. B; 25. True

BONUS
THE OSMONDS

The Osmonds were another group of brothers, this time from Utah, that began as a barbershop quartet. They originally began performing to earn money to help buy hearing aids for two of their brothers who were not in the group. They were later joined by their younger brothers, Jimmy and Donny. Both younger brothers would go on to release solo albums, with Donny becoming a heartthrob with his hit "Puppy Love."

1. True or False: The Osmonds were discovered at Disneyland, where the director of entertainment and customer relations found the brothers singing on Main Street.

2. The Osmonds started a variety act, appearing on variety shows by Andy Williams and what comedian?

A. Andy Griffith

B. Jerry Lewis

C. Sonny Bono

D. Lenny Bruce

3. The Osmonds went No. 1 on the pop charts for the first time with what song?

A. "One Bad Apple"

B. "Puppy Love"

C. "Sweet and Innocent"

D. "Go Away Little Girl"

4. Donny Osmond would go on to have a duo career with little sister Marie, including an eventual long-standing residency in Las Vegas. Over the years, how many studio albums did the brother/sister duo record together?

A. 5

B. 8

C. 7

D. 10

5. In which Broadway touring production did Donny Osmond perform as the lead character?

A. *Grease*

B. *Beauty and the Beast*

C. *Joseph and the Amazing Technicolor Dreamcoat*

D. *Waitress*

Answers: 1. True; 2. B; 3. A; 4. C; 5. C

1980s & 1990s

1980s & 1990s

New Edition

What started as two boys joining their friend on stage to support him because he was shy eventually grew into one of the most successful vocal groups of all time. New Edition came from humble backgrounds, but their hard work and dedication to their music helped them find worldwide success and adoring fans who love them and their songs to this day. While the group has taken breaks over the years, they always seem to come back to each other and to their fans, as they have since the late 1970s, when the guys were just friends in elementary school.

New Edition became a pioneering group of the late 1970s and early 1980s, influencing decades of fellow artists and boy bands. Their distinctive harmonies have given us some of the most endearing ballads, and hearing one of their biggest hits on the radio is sure to make any boy band fan smile.

New Edition

1. Where was New Edition formed?

A. Boston

B. Brooklyn

C. Compton

D. Houston

2. Which member of New Edition founded the band?

A. Ronnie DeVoe

B. Johnny Gill

C. Bobby Brown

D. Ricky Bell

3. What year did New Edition form?

A. 1975

B. 1978

C. 1976

D. 1977

4. True or False: The group called themselves New Edition because they were a "new edition" of the Jackson 5.

5. What is the name of the producer who originally wanted to sign Ralph Tresvant to a solo deal, but ended up signing the entire group?

A. Lou Pearlman
B. Johnny Wright
C. Maurice Starr
D. Simon Fuller

6. What was the name of New Edition's first single to go to No. 1?

A. "Can You Stand The Rain?"
B. "Candy Girl"
C. "Mr. Telephone Man"
D. "Hangin' Tough"

7. After their first major tour, the group was dropped off back at their families' homes with checks for how much money?

A. $1,500.59
B. $500,000
C. $18,000
D. $1.87

8. When New Edition fired Maurice Starr, what group did he create next?

A. Backstreet Boys

B. New Kids On The Block

C. Perfect Gentlemen

D. Hanson

9. After gaining new management and signing a new record deal, what was the name of the group's second album?

A. *New Edition*

B. *Cool It Now*

C. *All For Love*

D. *Count Me Out*

10. Which member of New Edition did the group vote out in 1985 due to the way he acted both on- and offstage?

A. Ricky Bell

B. Ronnie DeVoe

C. Bobby Brown

D. Michael Bivins

11. For which movie did New Edition rerecord a 1954 hit by the Penguins?

A. *License to Drive*

B. *The Karate Kid Part II*

C. *Back to the Future Part II*

D. *Baby Boom*

WE

12. What singer was added to the group in 1987?

A. Johnny Gill

B. Babyface

C. Lionel Richie

D. Jordan Knight

13. Which producers, known for working with Janet Jackson, did New Edition work with on their fifth album, *Heart Break*?

A. Nile Rogers and Simon LeBon

B. Rick Rubin and Mutt Lange

C. Mutt Lange and Max Martin

D. Jimmy Jam and Terry Lewis

14. Which former child actor directed and starred in the group's video for "N.E. Heart Break"?

A. Lisa Bonet

B. Malcolm Jamal Warner

C. Macaulay Culkin

D. Brooke Shields

15. What future vocal group named themselves after a song from New Edition's *Heart Break* album?

A. Backstreet Boys

B. NSYNC

C. Boyz II Men

D. 98 Degrees

16. Which pop queen did Bobby Brown marry in 1992?

A. Madonna

B. Whitney Houston

C. Paula Abdul

D. Debbie Gibson

17. Despite having a No. 1 song, Bobby Brown's debut solo album failed to gain traction. Which producer did Bobby not work with on his second and most successful solo album, *Don't Be Cruel*?

A. R. Kelly

B. Babyface

C. L.A. Reid

D. Teddy Riley

18. While New Edition took a break, Ricky Bell, Michael Bivins, and Ronnie DeVoe created a trio called Bell Biv DeVoe. What was the name of their first single?

A. "Do Me!"

B. "Poison"

C. "B.B.D. (I Thought It Was Me?)"

D. "She's Dope!"

19. **New Edition's music was considered "new jack swing," which contained elements of which music genres?**

A. Rap, R&B, and Funk
B. Country, R&B, and Rap
C. Funk, Pop, and R&B
D. Rap, Funk, and Rock

20. **What was the name of the New Edition album that was released in 1996—their first in eight years?**

A. *About Time*
B. *Home Again*
C. *Forever*
D. *Same Edition*

21. **Bobby Brown, Johnny Gill, and Ralph Tresvant joined singers Monica, Faith Evans, and Whitney Houston on "Somebody Bigger Than You and I." The song appeared in what movie?**

A. *The Bodyguard*
B. *The Princess Dairies*
C. *Cinderella*
D. *The Preacher's Wife*

22. In 2002, New Edition caught the eye of what producer and was signed to his Bad Boy Records label?

A. Sean "Puffy" Combs

B. R. Kelley

C. Jermaine Dupri

D. Timbaland

23. What reunited group did New Edition record the song "Full Service" with in 2008?

A. Boyz II Men

B. New Kids On The Block

C. NSYNC

D. The Jacksons

24. Where did all six members of New Edition reunite in July 2011 to celebrate their thirtieth anniversary?

A. Coachella

B. Music Midtown

C. iHeartRadio Music Festival

D. Essence Music Festival

25. What network aired *The New Edition Story*, a three-episode miniseries about the group, in 2017?

A. MTV

B. CBS

C. BET

D. VH1

Answers: 1. A; 2. C; 3. B; 4. True; 5. C; 6. B; 7. D; 8. B; 9. A; 10. C; 11. B; 12. A; 13. D; 14. B; 15. C; 16. B; 17. A; 18. B; 19. A; 20. B; 21. D; 22. A; 23. B; 24. D; 25. C

BONUS
MENUDO

Hailing from Puerto Rico, Menudo formed and began performing in 1977. They were a hit at home right off the bat but found international fame in 1981. Though they never reached the heights of groups like New Edition, they did make commercials for Burger King, Pepsi, and Crest. Known for retiring members when they got too old, the group's lineup has changed quite a bit over the years, but that just means there were more members for Menudo fans to fawn over!

1. Which well-known performer is also a former member of Menudo?

A. Mario Lopez

B. Ricky Martin

C. Marc Anthony

D. Bad Bunny

2. Menudo has been estimated to have sold how many albums worldwide?

A. 100 million

B. 50 million

C. 5 million

D. 20 million

3. True or False: Several former members of Menudo reunited in 1998 and 2019 and went by the name El Reencuentro.

4. Which '90s boy band member auditioned to be a part of Menudo?

A. Brian Littrell
B. AJ McLean
C. Howie Dorough
D. Chris Kirkpatrick

5. How many members of Menudo have there been since the group started in 1977?

A. 42
B. 37
C. 54
D. 25

Answers: 1. B; 2. D; 3. True; 4. C; 5. A

A

1980s & 1990s

NEW KIDS ON THE BLOCK

While their mothers and aunts had the Beatles growing up, girls in the mid-1980s had New Kids On The Block. The career of these five boys from Beantown started out slow but took off with a song from their second album.

They sold out concerts across the world and even had a Saturday morning cartoon show. Their faces were on bedsheets, lunchboxes, nightgowns, and toothbrushes. They inspired a new generation of boy bands heading into the 1990s. They became a part of catchy tunes by boy bands like LFO's "Summer Girl." The group took a break for more than a decade but is back now and stronger than ever. With sold-out tours, hit albums, and solo careers in music, film, and TV, New Kids On The Block aren't going anywhere anytime soon.

NEW KIDS ON THE BLOCK

1. **Who was the first member of New Kids On The Block?**

A. Donnie Wahlberg

B. Joey McIntyre

C. Jordan Knight

D. Danny Wood

2. **How are Jordan and Jonathan Knight related?**

A. First cousins

B. Uncle and nephew

C. Brothers

D. Second cousins

3. **True or False:** Actor Mark Wahlberg, Donnie's younger brother, was originally a member of New Kids On The Block.

4. What was the band's original name?

A. BlockStreet

B. Nynuk

C. Bean Town Boys

D. New Kids On Your Street

5. How did the group get the name New Kids On The Block?

A. A neighbor in Dorchester

B. Maurice Starr's brother

C. A song Donnie wrote on their first album

D. The name of their favorite movie

6. What was the name of New Kids On The Block's first single?

A. "Be My Girl"

B. "Stop It Girl"

C. "Popsicle"

D. "Didn't I (Blow Your Mind?)"

7. While their self-titled debut album failed to gain any national attention, their label, Columbia, let them record a second album. What is the name of that album?

A. *Step By Step*

B. *Please Don't Go Girl*

C. *Tonight*

D. *Hangin' Tough*

8. **The first single from the second album, "Please Don't Go Girl," did not do well. However, just before the group was going to be let go from their label, a DJ in which state played the song, turning it into an eventual hit?**

A. Tennessee

B. Kansas

C. Florida

D. Georgia

9. **After the success of "Please Don't Go Girl," New Kids On The Block was asked to open for what pop star (only to have her open for them when they went on their second tour)?**

A. Tiffany

B. Debbie Gibson

C. Whitney Houston

D. Janet Jackson

10. **After their single, "You Got It (the Right Stuff)," became a hit on MTV, their next single became their first No. 1 on the *Billboard* charts. What song was it?**

A. "Cover Girl"

B. "Didn't I (Blow Your Mind)?"

C. "I'll Be Loving You (Forever)"

D. "This One's for the Children"

11. For "Step By Step," in what order did the members sing their "steps" in the bridge of the song?

A. Danny, Donnie, Jordan, Joe, Jon

B. Donnie, Jordan, Danny, Joe, Jon

C. Jordan, Jon, Joey, Danny, Donnie

D. Joey, Donnie, Danny, Jordan, Jon

12. What was the name of the tour the group went on after the release of their fourth album, *Step By Step*?

A. The Tonight Tour

B. The Summer Magic Tour

C. No More Games Tour

D. The Hangin' Tough Again Tour

13. What was the phone number for the Official New Kids On The Block Hotline?

A. 1-900-955-KIDS

B. 1-900-909-5KIDS

C. 1-800-905-5NEW

D. 1-800-909-KIDS

14. In 1993, New Kids On The Block shortened their name to what?

A. New Kids

B. The Block

C. NKOTB

D. Kids Block

15. What year did New Kids On The Block break up?

A. 1992
B. 1990
C. 1994
D. 1999

16. Which New Kid released a solo album first?

A. Joey
B. Jordan
C. Danny
D. Donnie

17. True or False: After two former NKOTB members released solo albums in 1999, MTV tried to reunite the group for their Video Music Awards, but Jonathan was the only member who didn't want to do it.

18. New Kids On The Block announced their reunion on April 4, 2008, on what television morning show?

A. *Regis and Kathy Lee*
B. *Good Morning America*
C. *Fox and Friends*
D. *The Today Show*

19. Which R&B singer performed on the group's second single, "Single," from their 2008 album *The Block*?

A. Usher

B. Mario

C. Ne-Yo

D. Bruno Mars

20. What hit television show was mentioned in the lyrics of "2 in the Morning"?

A. *Friends*

B. *Molly & Mike*

C. *Grey's Anatomy*

D. *Stranger Things*

21. Which boy band did New Kids On The Block team up with for a 2011/2012 world tour?

A. 98 Degrees

B. Boyz II Men

C. Backstreet Boys

D. Big Time Rush

22. What happened to New Kids On The Block on June 22, 2012?

A. They received a star on the Hollywood Walk of Fame

B. They released a new album

C. They announced they were touring again with the Backstreet Boys

D. They won a Grammy Award

23. On April 2, 2013, New Kids On The Block released their seventh studio album. What was it called?

A. *The Block, Part 2*

B. *10*

C. *The Remix*

D. *Boys in the Band*

24. Which performer has New Kids On The Block not toured with since their reunion?

A. Debbie Gibson

B. Paula Abdul

C. Tiffany

D. Cyndi Lauper

25. Which baseball field has New Kids On The Block played sold-out shows at since their reunion?

A. Truist Park

B. Fenway Park

C. Yankees Stadium

D. Citi Field

Answers: 1. A; 2. C; 3. True; 4. B; 5. C; 6. A; 7. D; 8. C; 9. A; 10. C; 11. A; 12. B; 13. B; 14. C; 15. C; 16. A; 17. True; 18. D; 19. C; 20. C; 21. C; 22. A; 23. B; 24. D; 25. B

BONUS
COLOR ME BADD

Color Me Badd formed in 1985, around the same time as New Kids On The Block, but their rise to fame was a bit different. After close calls with celebrity, like getting the chance to open for Bon Jovi after running into Jon Bon Jovi in a movie theater, they moved to New York in 1989. There they met producers Jimmy Jam and Terry Lewis, who advised them on their next career move. The band wrote what would become one of their most popular songs and landed a record deal.

1. Where are the members of Color Me Badd originally from?

A. Georgia

B. Tennessee

C. Oklahoma

D. New Jersey

2. Where did the band get their name?

A. A misspelling on a contract

B. A horse at the racetrack

C. They just wanted to look different

D. Graffiti on the side of a building

3. Their first single became the biggest hit on the New Jack City soundtrack. What was the name of the song?

A. "All 4 Love"

B. "I Adore Mi Amor"

C. "Slow Motion"

D. "I Wanna Sex You Up"

4. Color Me Badd made a cameo appearance on what hit television show in 1992, when some of the characters tried to track them down in a hotel?

A. *Melrose Place*

B. *Beverly Hills, 90210*

C. *Saved by the Bell*

D. *California Dreams*

5. True or False: Color Me Badd was inducted into the Oklahoma Music Hall of Fame in 2000.

Answers: 1. C; 2. B; 3. D; 4. B; 5. True

1980s & 1990s

Boyz II Men

With harmonies smoother than butter, Boyz II Men took the world by storm in the early 1990s. The group hailed from Philadelphia, the land of *Rocky*, cheesesteaks, and some of the most important moments in American history. Unlike others during that era, the group has stood the test of time, still performing nearly forty years after they began. Their vocal prowess and the emotional depth in their songs have made them legends in the music industry.

While New Kids On The Block may have inspired later boy bands and the surrounding fangirl phenomenon, Boyz II Men inspired the tight, timeless harmonies that make boy bands unique. They are the reason why boy bands after them took their vocals so seriously—they all wanted to sound like Boyz II Men. Their enduring love songs are still popular today, as is the group itself.

Boyz II Men

1. Who was the first member of Boyz II Men?

A. Nathan Morris
B. Michael McCary
C. Wanya Morris
D. Shawn Stockman

2. What was Boyz II Men's original name?

A. Real Boyz
B. Unique Attraction
C. BoyzSong
D. Opposites Attract

3. True or False: Boyz II Men was trying to find Will Smith at a concert in Philadelphia, to perform for him in hopes of getting a record deal, when they ran into Michael Bivins of New Edition/Bel Biv DeVoe instead. He gave them his card.

4. Boyz II Men's first album, *Cooleyhighharmoney*, was released on what record label?

A. MCA
B. Motown
C. Arista
D. Jive

5. Which member performed the bass and spoken-word parts of songs?

A. Wanya Morris
B. Nathan Morris
C. Shawn Stockman
D. Michael McCary

6. What musician and fellow alumni of the Philadelphia High School for Creative and Performing Arts cameoed in the music video of "Motownphilly"?

A. Will Smith

B. Seal

C. Questlove

D. Mariah Carey

7. True or False: Boyz II Men won Best New Artist at the 1992 Grammy Awards.

8. Which song did Boyz II Men record for the 1992 Eddie Murphy movie *Boomerang*?

A. "End of the Road"

B. "On Bended Knee"

C. "It's So Hard To Say Goodbye To Yesterday"

D. "Uhh Ahh"

9. Which single remained at No. 1 on the *Billboard* Hot 100 chart for thirteen weeks?

A. "On Bended Knee"

B. "I'll Make Love To You"

C. "End of the Road"

D. "Water Runs Dry"

10. True or False: When *Cooleyhighharmoney* was rereleased internationally, "End of the Road" was not included.

11. What was the name of Boyz II Men's 1993 Christmas album?

A. *Christmas Interpretations*

B. *It's Christmas Time*

C. *Christmas in Philly*

D. *Merry Christmas*

12. The group's second release, *II*, sold how many albums in 1994 in the United States alone?

A. 5 million

B. 20 million

C. 12 million

D. 10 million

13. Which song broke the thirteen-week record that Boyz II Men held for having a song at No. 1?

A. Mariah Carey, "Always Be My Baby"

B. Whitney Houston, "I Will Always Love You"

C. New Kids On The Block, "Dirty Dawg"

D. Boyz II Men, "I'll Make Love To You"

14. Boyz II Men is only the third artist to replace themselves at No. 1 on the *Billboard* Hot 100 charts. Who were the other two?

A. New Kids On The Block and Whitney Houston

B. Elvis Presley and the Beatles

C. The Beatles and Whitney Houston

D. Elvis Presley and New Kids On The Block

15. Boyz II Men created their own record label. What was it called?

A. Stonecreek

B. Riverwood

C. Stonehenge

D. River Rose

16. Which actress was *not* a star of the group's "On Bended Knee" music video?

A. Lark Voorhies

B. Victoria Rowell

C. Tisha Campbell

D. Kim Fields

17. "A Song for Mama" from the album *Evolution* was produced by Babyface and appears on what movie soundtrack?

A. *Soul Food*

B. *The Preacher's Wife*

C. *Waiting to Exhale*

D. *Poetic Justice*

18. Which member of the group left the band in 2003 due to chronic back problems and multiple sclerosis?

A. Wanya

B. Michael

C. Shawn

D. Nathan

19. What is *not* the name of an album that Boyz II Men released between 2004 and 2008?

A. *Motown: A Journey Through Hitsville USA*

B. *Apocalypse*

C. *Heaven*

D. *The Remedy*

20. Boyz II Men's 2009 album, *Love*, featured covers of love songs from various artists, such as Lonestar's "Amazed," Cyndi Lauper's "Time After Time," and Take That's "Back for Good." Which former *American Idol* judge produced the album with the group?

A. Paula Abdul

B. Randy Jackson

C. Simon Cowell

D. Mariah Carey

21. Boyz II Men joined which fellow boy bands for the 2013 Package Tour?

A. Backstreet Boys and New Kids On The Block

B. 98 Degrees and Backstreet Boys

C. New Kids On The Block and Take That

D. 98 Degrees and New Kids On The Block

22. What popular sitcom did Boyz II Men appear on in 2013, to sing an a cappella version of "You Just Got Slapped"?

A. *How I Met Your Mother*

B. *The Big Bang Theory*

C. *The Office*

D. *Parks and Recreation*

23. What song did Boyz II Men sing in the 2016 version of *Grease Live!*?

A. "Summer Lovin'"

B. "Hopelessly Devoted To You"

C. "Sandy"

D. "Beauty School Dropout"

24. Which member of Boyz II Men placed fourth on *Dancing with the Stars* in 2016?

A. Michael

B. Shawn

C. Wanya

D. Nathan

25. Which two members of Boyz II Men took part in ABC's 2021 special, *A Very Boy Band Christmas*, with members of NSYNC, 98 Degrees, O-Town, and more?

A. Wanya and Nathan

B. Nathan and Shawn

C. Shawn and Michael

D. Wanya and Shawn

Answers: 1. A; 2. B; 3. True; 4. B; 5. D; 6. C; 7. False; 8. A; 9. C; 10. False; 11. A; 12. C; 13. D; 14. B; 15. A; 16. C; 17. A; 18. B; 19. C; 20. B; 21. D; 22. A; 23. D; 24. C; 25. D

BONUS
ALL-4-ONE

All-4-One, a four-part vocal harmony group and boy band from the Antelope Valley and Mojave areas of California, came together in 1993 and quickly made a name for themselves. During the height of Boyz II Men's reign as kings of vocal harmony groups, All-4-One won Grammys and had both No. 1 singles and platinum albums. Like most groups, they went their separate ways after problems with record labels, but they began performing again as a group in the 2010s to adoring fans everywhere.

1. All-4-One's songs "I Swear" and "I Can Love You Like That" were covered by which country singer?

A. Luke Bryan

B. John Michael Montgomery

C. Garth Brooks

D. Alan Jackson

2. For which Disney animated film did All-4-One record the song "Someday"?

A. *The Hunchback of Notre Dame*

B. *The Lion King*

C. *The Rescuers Down Under*

D. *A Goofy Movie*

3. Which member of All-4-One is a cofounder of the Catalina Film Festival?

A. Jamie Jones

B. Tony Borowiak

C. Alfred Nevarez

D. Tim Kennedy

4. True or False: All-4-One released their eighth studio album, *Twenty+*, in 2015.

5. In 2016, All-4-One joined what tour, which also featured Vanilla Ice, Color Me Badd, and Young MC?

A. The Block Party

B. I Love the 90s

C. 90s Con

D. The Total Package Tour

Answers: 1. B; 2. A; 3. D; 4. True; 5. B

1980s & 1990s

take that

While Boyz II Men was just getting noticed in the United States, over in Manchester, England, five guys were forming a pop group that would end up taking the United Kingdom by storm. There was a manager named Nigel Martin-Smith who wanted to create a group like other successful acts of the time—sound familiar?—and sought five young performers in the New Kids On The Block vein. Take That quickly began making television appearances across the UK on shows such as *The Hitman and Her*, performing unreleased songs that fit into the new jack swing genre that was popular in the United States. After a few minor hits, the group won the hearts of fans across the UK and Europe. Take That played a significant role in shaping boy bands of the future, especially in the United Kingdom. Take That is not just a boy band—they are a cherished part of people's lives.

1980s & 1990s

take that

1. Who was the first member of Take That?

A. Howard Donald

B. Gary Barlow

C. Jason Orange

D. Robbie Williams

2. Who was the youngest member of Take That when they joined at sixteen?

A. Robbie Williams

B. Jason Orange

C. Mark Owen

D. Gary Barlow

3. What was the name of the song, written by Gary Barlow, that Take That performed on *The Hitman and Her* in their first television appearance?

A. "Once You've Tasted Love"

B. "Promises"

C. "Do What U Like"

D. "My Kind of Girl"

4. True or False: In June 1993, the group recorded a cover of the 1975 hit, "It Only Takes a Minute," which peaked at No. 7 on the UK singles chart. It was June 1992.

5. What Barry Manilow cover did the group record and release that hit No. 3 on the UK singles chart?

A. "Could It Be Magic"

B. "Copacabana"

C. "Mandy"

D. "Weekend in New England"

6. What was the name of Take That's first album?

A. *Take That*

B. *Take That and Party*

C. *Suck It Up and Take That*

D. *Take That Magic*

7. In 1993, Take That's second album, *Everything Changes*, was released and gave the group their first four consecutive No. 1 singles. Which song was not one of those No. 1 songs?

A. "Relight My Fire"

B. "Babe"

C. "Everything Changes"

D. "Why Can't I Wake Up with You"

8. What is the name of Take That's biggest hit to date, which was also their only hit in the United States?

A. "Sure"

B. "Back for Good"

C. "Pray"

D. "Babe"

9. The cover for the group's third album, *Nobody Else*, is a parody of what famous album cover?

A. The Beatles' *Sgt. Pepper's Lonely Hearts Club*

B. Nirvana's *Nevermind*

C. Fleetwood Mac's *Rumours*

D. The Beatles' *Abbey Road*

10. Who was the first member of Take That to leave?

A. Gary Barlow

B. Howard Donald

C. Robbie Williams

D. Jason Orange

11. After the group agreed to disband in 1996, they released a greatest hits album that featured what cover of a Bee Gees hit?

A. "Stayin' Alive"

B. "How Deep Is Your Love?"

C. "Night Fever"

D. "More Than A Woman"

12. Gary Barlow released his first solo songs the same year that Take That disbanded. What was the name of his first single?

A. "Love Won't Wait"

B. "Open Road"

C. "Forever Love"

D. "Are You Ready Now?"

13. Robbie Williams's first solo single after leaving Take That was a cover of which George Michael song?

A. "Faith"

B. "Freedom"

C. "One More Try"

D. "Father Figure"

14. True or False: "Angels," Robbie Williams's fourth single from his debut album, *Life thru a Lens*, became his biggest hit in the United Kingdom, making his album the fifty-eighth best-selling album in UK history.

15. After taking part in a TV special to talk about Take That's success and releasing a new hits compilation in 2005, the remaining four members of the group announced that they would tour the next year. What was the name of the tour?

A. Beautiful World Tour
B. The Ultimate Tour
C. Never Forget Tour
D. Relight My Fire Tour

16. Take That's comeback single, "Patience," peaked at what position on the charts?

A. No. 1
B. No. 5
C. No. 8
D. No. 12

17. **Take That's song "Rule the World" was recorded for what soundtrack?**

A. *Spider-Man 3*

B. *Stardust*

C. *Ghost Rider*

D. *Across the Universe*

18. **In 2010, Gary Barlow and Robbie Williams worked together for the first time since 1995 on a song for Robbie's next solo album. What was the name of the song?**

A. "The English"

B. "Shame"

C. "Progressive"

D. "Shine"

19. **Robbie Williams announced his return to Take That in July 2010, and the band released which album that November?**

A. *Progress*

B. *Heart and I*

C. *Never Forget*

D. *Got to Dance*

20. **In 2011, Take That's first tour together as a fivesome since 1995 sold how many tickets in one day?**

A. 800,000

B. 2,500,000

C. 1,100,000

D. 750,000

21. Why did Robbie Williams not join Take That in performing during the closing ceremonies of the 2012 Summer Olympics in London?

A. He quit the band

B. His wife was having a baby

C. He got sick

D. He was in a car accident

22. Which two members left the band in 2014 before the release of their next album?

A. Gary and Howard

B. Robbie and Mark

C. Mark and Jason

D. Robbie and Jason

23. What was the name of Take That's first single as a trio?

A. "These Days"

B. "Forever"

C. "Hey Boy"

D. "Three"

24. Where did Take That perform on May 7, 2023?

A. At a children's hospital

B. As part of Taylor Swift's Eras Tour

C. At King Charles III's coronation concert

D. On ITV

25. What show about a group of British teens features an episode where the teens sneak into a Take That concert in Belfast in 1993?

A. *Derry Girls*

B. *Gregory's Girl*

C. *A Woman of Substance*

D. *Sex Education*

Answers: 1. B; 2. A; 3. D; 4. False; 5. A; 6. B; 7. D; 8. B; 9. A; 10. C; 11. B; 12. C; 13. B; 14. True; 15. B; 16. A; 17. B; 18. B; 19. A; 20. C; 21. B; 22. D; 23. A; 24. C; 25. A

BONUS BOYZONE

After forming in 1993, Boyzone often rode the same wave of fame as Take That. In fact, the band came together after an ad in a newspaper that was taken out by a man who wanted to form an "Irish Take That." The group broke up and got back together twice (1993–2000 and 2007–2019) but gave us one of the most successful solo careers from a boy band with Ronan Keating.

1. What was the name of Boyzone's first album?

A. *Everything Is Now*
B. *Said and Done*
C. *So Good*
D. *Shooting Star*

2. True or False: Boyzone's first album went to No. 1 on the charts in Ireland and the UK.

3. Boyzone received their first No. 1 song in the United Kingdom with a remake of what song?

A. "I'd Do Anything For Love (But I Won't Do That)" by Meat Loaf
B. "Words" by the Bee Gees
C. "Hey Jude" by the Beatles
D. "Uptown Girl" by Billy Joel

4. Boyzone member Ronan Keating recorded a cover of the country song "When You Say Nothing At All." In which movie did this song appear?

A. *Four Weddings and a Funeral*

B. *Bridget Jones's Diary*

C. *Notting Hill*

D. *Sense and Sensibility*

5. Which member of Boyzone passed away on October 10, 2009?

A. Shane Lynch

B. Ronan Keating

C. Stephen Gately

D. Keith Duffy

Answers: 1. B; 2. True; 3. B; 4. C; 5. C

BOYS
BSB
treet
Boys

1980s & 1990s

BACKSTREET BOYS

The Backstreet Boys are the best-selling boy band of all time, with over 130 million albums sold. The group of five guys from both Florida and Kentucky began their trek to stardom in an enchanted place: Orlando, Florida. It was a slow start to stardom, before they made their way over to Europe, where they first hit it big. Eventually, the group became famous in Canada, and that fame dripped down to the United States. Then there was no stopping the Backstreet Boys.

The group celebrated their thirtieth anniversary in 2023 and they have no plans to stop. Their music has the power to transport you back to a time when you had no worries, which is probably why their arena concerts still sell out thirty years later. Their timeless music and harmonies never waver, and they still have the outgoing personalities they had as teenagers all these years later.

Like the line from one of their most famous songs, people like to say that "Backstreet's back." But the truth is, they never left.

BACKSTREET

1. Who was the first, original Backstreet Boy?

A. Nick Carter

B. AJ McLean

C. Howie Dorough

D. Kevin Richardson

2. What was the name of the man who put an ad in the *Orlando Sentinel* looking for a "New Kids On The Block" type band?

A. Johnny Wright

B. Maurice Starr

C. Lou Pearlman

D. Carl Sanders

3. What was the stage name that Howie Dorough used to audition for the Backstreet Boys?

A. Tony Donetti

B. Johnny Suede

C. Mario Martin

D. Robert Ringwald

4. Where did the group get the name Backstreet Boys?

A. They grew up on a back street

B. An international market in Orlando

C. A combination of their first and last names

D. The name of the street where Lou Pearlman's offices were

5. When and where did the Backstreet Boys perform for the public for the first time?

A. May 1, 1992, at Lou Pearlman's birthday party

B. July 4, 1993, at a local radio station celebration

C. May 8, 1993, at SeaWorld's Grad Nite

D. April 20, 1993, at Disney World

6. What record label considered signing the Backstreet Boys before the band signed with Jive Records?

A. MCA Records

B. Mercury Records

C. Arista Records

D. LaFace Records

7. The Backstreet Boys began working with producers Denniz PoP and Max Martin in Sweden for their first album. What other well-known group was the producing duo known for working with at the time?

A. NSYNC

B. Boyz II Men

C. Ace of Base

D. The Beatles

8. What was the name of the Backstreet Boys' first single?

A. "Quit Playing Games (With My Heart)"

B. "As Long as You Love Me"

C. "Tell Me That I'm Dreaming"

D. "We've Got It Goin' On"

9. In what country did the Backstreet Boys earn their first platinum album?

A. Germany

B. United States

C. Canada

D. United Kingdom

10. Which song was on the international edition of Backstreet Boys, the group's self-titled debut album, but *not* on the US edition?

A. "We've Got It Goin' On"

B. "Missing You"

C. "Just to Be Close to You"

D. "Anywhere for You"

11. In the chorus of "As Long as You Love Me," the Backstreet Boys "don't care" about a few things. Which is *not* one of those things?

A. Where you're from

B. Who you are

C. Where you go

D. What you did

12. What song did the Backstreet Boys perform at the 1998 MTV Video Music Awards?

A. "Everybody (Backstreet's Back)"

B. "Larger Than Life"

C. "Quit Playing Games (With My Heart)"

D. "I'll Never Break Your Heart"

13. Which Backstreet Boy had open heart surgery in May 1998?

A. Nick Carter

B. AJ McLean

C. Brian Littrell

D. Howie Dorough

14. **On what date did the city of Orlando first name Backstreet Boys Day?**

A. October 14, 1998

B. October 1, 1997

C. October 8, 1999

D. October 7, 1998

15. **How many copies did the 1999 album *Millennium* sell in the first week?**

A. 1,843,000

B. 1,134,000

C. 2,142,000

D. 2,433,000

16. Which song was *not* a single from *Millennium*?

A. "The One"

B. "Show Me the Meaning of Being Lonely"

C. "Larger Than Life"

D. "Don't Want You Back"

17. Which song was featured on the Backstreet Boys' *For the Fans* CDs that were sold at Burger King to promote their 2000 album, *Black & Blue*?

A. "It's True"

B. "How Did I Fall in Love with You?"

C. "More Than That"

D. "10,000 Promises"

18. True or False: The Backstreet Boys performed at the Super Bowl XXXV halftime show on January 28, 2021.

19. Why was the Black & Blue Tour put on hold on July 9, 2001?

A. Nick broke his leg

B. AJ went into rehab

C. Kevin needed a break

D. Howie went solo

20. What talk show did AJ McLean's bandmates surprise him on in November 2003?

A. *The Tonight Show*

B. *The Late Show with David Letterman*

C. *The Oprah Winfrey Show*

D. *The Wendy Williams Show*

21. Which member of the Backstreet Boys announced that he was leaving the band in June 2006?

A. Kevin Richardson

B. AJ McLean

C. Howie Dorough

D. Brian Littrell

22. Which Backstreet Boys hit was *not* part of the *NKOTBSB* compilation album?

A. "I Want It That Way"

B. "Quit Playing Games (With My Heart)"

C. "Shape of My Heart"

D. "As Long as You Love Me"

23. Where did the Backstreet Boys have their first real performance as a group after Kevin Richardson's return?

A. *Good Morning America*
B. *The Oprah Winfrey Show*
C. *The Tonight Show*
D. *Live with Regis and Kelly*

24. What happened to the Backstreet Boys on April 22, 2013?

A. They celebrated their twenty-fifth anniversary
B. They released their new album
C. They received their star on the Hollywood Walk of Fame
D. They won their first Grammy Award

25. *In a World Like This*, the Backstreet Boys' eighth studio album, was released on the group's independent record label. What is that label called?

A. Show 'Em Records
B. N-KAHB
C. K-BAHN
D. Backstreet Records

Answers: 1. B; 2. C; 3. A; 4. B; 5. C; 6. B; 7. C; 8. D; 9. A; 10. B; 11. C; 12. A; 13. C; 14. D; 15. B; 16. D; 17. A; 18. False; 19. B; 20. C; 21. A; 22. C; 23. A; 24. C; 25. C

BONUS WESTLIFE

The members of Irish boy band Westlife came together as students at Summerhill College, after performing in a production of *Grease* in 1997, around the same time that the Backstreet Boys had already won over Europe and were just breaking into the United States. After a few changes to the Westlife lineup, the group came together in 1998 and quickly signed a record deal with MCA Records.

1. What was Westlife's original name?

A. Six of One
B. Six as One
C. One of Six
D. Five of Six

2. Who did Westlife open for in Dublin in 1998 (an opportunity that they called their big break)?

A. NSYNC and the Backstreet Boys
B. Take That and Boyz II Men
C. Backstreet Boys and Boyzone
D. Boyzone and NSYNC

3. Which song did the group cover with Mariah Carey in 2000?

A. "I Will Always Love You"

B. "My Love"

C. "When You Say Nothing at All"

D. "Against All Odds (Take a Look at Me Now)"

4. Which member left the band in 2004?

A. Brian McFadden

B. Kian Egan

C. Shane Filan

D. Mark Feehily

5. In August 2023, Westlife announced their first tour dates in which two countries?

A. China and South Korea

B. United States and Canada

C. Mexico and United States

D. Canada and South Korea

Answers: 1. B; 2. C; 3. D; 4. A; 5. B

1980s & 1990s

NSYNC

After coming together in the land of boy band dreams, Orlando, Florida, the guys of NSYNC followed the same route as the Backstreet Boys. Working with producers in Sweden, the group gained a following in Europe before eventually breaking into the United States in 1998 thanks to a Disney Channel special that was first offered to their counterparts.

NSYNC's success is not just attributed to their musical talent but also to their electrifying stage presence. Their synchronized dance routines and dynamic performances set a new standard for live shows, captivating audiences around the world. The energy and enthusiasm they brought to the stage created an infectious atmosphere of joy and excitement. Their impact goes beyond the realm of music, as they became cultural icons who transcended the boy band label.

That was just the beginning for the group that would give the world Justin Timberlake.

NSYNC

1. Which show did JC Chasez and Justin Timberlake star on?

A. *American Bandstand*

B. *The Mickey Mouse Club*

C. *Kids Incorporated*

D. *You Can't Do That on Television*

2. How did members Joey Fatone and Chris Kirkpatrick know one another?

A. They went to college together

B. They attended the same church

C. They both worked at Universal Studios

D. Their mothers were best friends

3. Who was the last member of NSYNC to join the band?

A. Joey Fatone

B. JC Chasez

C. Justin Timberlake

D. Lance Bass

4. True or False: Chris Kirkpatrick was originally up for a spot in the Backstreet Boys.

5. Who came up with the name NSYNC (which is made up of the last letter in each original member's first name)?

A. Lou Pearlman

B. JC's father

C. Justin's mother

D. Lance Bass

6. Which member of NSYNC sings in falsetto?

A. Joey

B. Chris

C. Lance

D. Justin

7. Where did NSYNC hold their first public performance?

A. Pleasure Island

B. Downtown Disney

C. Epcot Center

D. Church Street Station

8. The European version of NSYNC's first album included a cover of which 1980s hit?

A. "Don't Stop Believin'"

B. "More Than a Feeling"

C. "Billie Jean"

D. "Nothing's Gonna Stop Us Now"

9. What was NSYNC's first single in the United States and in Germany?

A. "Here We Go"

B. "I Drive Myself Crazy"

C. "I Want You Back"

D. "Tearin' Up My Heart"

10. Due to the success of the Disney Channel concert and their album's rise on the charts, who did the group begin opening for on their tour?

A. Mariah Carey

B. Janet Jackson

C. Madonna

D. Shania Twain

11. Which *Friends* star had a part in the *Armageddon* spoof, *Armagedd'NSync*, for the 1999 MTV Movie & TV Awards?

A. Lisa Kudrow

B. Courtney Cox

C. Jennifer Aniston

D. Matthew Perry

12. Chris launched a fashion line in 1999. What was it called?

A. Pineapple Head

B. FuMan Shoelace

C. NSYNCO

D. FuMan Skeeto

13. When was the album *No Strings Attached* released?

A. May 1, 2000

B. March 21, 2000

C. May 12, 2000

D. March 2, 2000

14. Which two members of NSYNC were the first to star in a movie (2001's *On the Line*)?

A. JC and Justin

B. Lance and JC

C. Chris and Joey

D. Joey and Lance

15. Which NSYNC song is the only song of theirs to hit No. 1 on the *Billboard* Hot 100?

A. "It's Gonna Be Me"

B. "Bye Bye Bye"

C. "Girlfriend"

D. "I Want You Back"

16. What was the third and final single from *No Strings Attached*?

A. "Space Cowboy"

B. "It's Gonna Be Me"

C. "That's When I'll Stop Loving You"

D. "This I Promise You"

17. Which pop star did Justin Timberlake date from 1999 to 2002?

A. Christina Aguilera

B. Britney Spears

C. Jessica Simpson

D. Mandy Moore

18. NSYNC's third album, *Celebrity*, featured the hit "Pop." Who wrote the song?

A. Justin Timberlake and Wade Robson

B. JC Chasez and Wade Robson

C. JC Chasez and BT

D. Justin Timberlake and JC Chasez

19. Who was the first member of NSYNC to go solo?

A. JC

B. Lance

C. Justin

D. Chris

20. True or False: NSYNC officially broke up on July 11, 2003.

21. Which member of NSYNC went on to write and produce songs for the Backstreet Boys?

A. Joey

B. JC

C. Chris

D. Lance

22. Which two members of NSYNC were on *Dancing with the Stars*?

A. JC and Lance

B. Lance and Chris

C. Joey and Lance

D. JC and Chris

23. True or False: Joey Fatone and Chris Kirkpatrick starred in *Dead 7*, a zombie movie written by Backstreet Boy Nick Carter that also starred members of the Backstreet Boys, O-Town, and 98 Degrees.

24. Which pop princess did Joey, JC, Lance, and Chris perform with during Coachella in 2019?

A. Miley Cyrus

B. Olivia Rodrigo

C. Doja Cat

D. Ariana Grande

25. For which movie did the group reunite to record a new song in 2023?

A. *Trolls Band Together*

B. *Barbie*

C. *Reptile*

D. *Together Forever*

Answers: 1. B; 2. C; 3. D; 4. True; 5. C; 6. B; 7. A; 8. B; 9. C; 10. B; 11. A; 12. D; 13. B; 14. D; 15. A; 16. D; 17. B; 18. A; 19. C; 20. False; 21. B; 22. C; 23. True; 24. D; 25. A

BONUS
5IVE

The British boy band known as 5ive formed in 1997. They enjoyed success in Europe and Asia, but also had a hit in the United States. Known for their energetic performances and catchy tunes, 5ive's music became an anthem for a generation. The group's blend of pop and rap elements set them apart, and their dynamic stage presence made them unforgettable.

1. What other famous group was founded by the same creators of 5ive?

A. TLC

B. BTS

C. Spice Girls

D. Soul Decision

2. 5ive toured with which of their boy band predecessor in the '90s?

A. NSYNC

B. New Kids On The Block

C. Boyz II Men

D. Backstreet Boys

3. Which of the 5ive band members dated Melanie C (Sporty Spice)?

A. Ritchie

B. Jason

C. Abz

D. Scott

4. 5ive reunited following a hiatus during The Big Reunion tour in which year?

A. 2006

B. 2008

C. 2013

D. 2018

5. How many members of 5ive are there currently?

A. 3

B. 4

C. 5

D. 6

Answers: 1. C; 2. A; 3. B; 4. C; 5. A

98°
98°
98°
98°

98°

There were the Backstreet Boys and NSYNC, and then there was 98 Degrees. Unlike their predecessors, 98 Degrees formed by themselves, without the help of an older, rich businessman. The group came together through various connections and eventually found their way to Motown Records, the first label of their idols, Boyz II Men.

Their popularity peaked during the late 1990s and early 2000s, and then, to the chagrin of their fans, went on hiatus. The group reunited in 2012 and has continued to tour and release new music. Today, 98 Degrees remains celebrated for their smooth harmonies, romantic ballads, and contribution to the pop and R&B landscape. The group has maintained a dedicated fan base since the beginning and is remembered as one of the prominent boy bands of their era.

98°

1. Who was the founding member of 98 Degrees?

A. Jeff Timmons

B. Nick Lachey

C. Drew Lachey

D. Justin Jeffre

2. What was Drew Lachey's job in New York City when he got the call to join the band?

A. Actor in an Off-Broadway play

B. Janitor at MTV

C. Emergency medical technician

D. Radio DJ

3. What was Nick Lachey going to college for before joining the group?

A. Dentistry

B. Psychology

C. Cosmetology

D. Sports medicine

4. What was one of the possible band names that 98 Degrees rejected?

A. Buckeyes

B. Next Issue

C. 32 Degrees

D. Hot Pockets

5. What was the name of 98 Degrees' first single?

A. "Invisible Man"

B. "I Thought She Knew"

C. "True to Your Heart"

D. "Don't Wanna Lose You Now"

6. Who did 98 Degrees open for while promoting their first album?

A. Paula Abdul

B. Madonna

C. Alanis Morrisette

D. Janet Jackson

7. For which Disney movie did 98 Degrees team up with Stevie Wonder to record "True to Your Heart"?

A. *The Parent Trap*

B. *Mulan*

C. *Hercules*

D. *Tarzan*

8. What is the name of 98 Degrees' second album?

A. *98 Degrees and Rising*

B. *The Hardest Thing*

C. *True to Your Heart*

D. *Because of You*

9. What was the name of 98 Degrees' first big hit, which went to No. 3 on the Billboard US Hot 100 chart?

A. "The Hardest Thing"

B. "Because of You"

C. "If She Only Knew"

D. "Fly with Me"

10. What activity are the 98 Degrees members doing in the "The Hardest Thing" music video?

A. Auto racing

B. Football

C. Golf

D. Boxing

11. Who appeared at the end of the "I Do (Cherish You)" music video as the groom?

A. Paul Reubens

B. Will Smith

C. Dustin Diamond

D. Bob Barker

12. The group earned their first No. 1 with the song "Thank God I Found You," a collaboration with R&B singer Joe and which pop icon?

A. Whitney Houston

B. Mariah Carey

C. Madonna

D. Tina Turner

13. The group's next album, *Revelation*, peaked at what number on the charts?

A. No. 2

B. No. 5

C. No. 10

D. No. 4

14. True or False: Nick Lachey wrote "My Everything" about Britney Spears.

15. Which member of the group is kidnapped in the "Give Me Just One Night (Una Noche)" music video?

A. Nick Lachey

B. Justin Jeffre

C. Drew Lachey

D. No one

16. What year did 98 Degrees go on hiatus?

A. 2002

B. 2005

C. 2003

D. 2009

17. In which TV show did Nick Lachey have a recurring role?

A. *True Blood*

B. *Charmed*

C. *Beverly Hills, 90210*

D. *Friends*

18. Which 98 Degrees member won the second season of *Dancing with the Stars*?

A. Justin Jeffre

B. Nick Lachey

C. Drew Lachey

D. Jeff Timmons

19. What was the name of Jeff Timmons's solo album?

A. *Whisper That Way*

B. *Favorite Star*

C. *Angel Eyes*

D. *That Day*

20. What former Miss Teen South Carolina, actress, and MTV VJ starred in Nick Lachey's music video, "What's Left Of Me," and later became his second wife?

A. Hilarie Burton

B. Vanessa Minnillo

C. Sophia Bush

D. Gisele Bündchen

21. Which 98 Degrees member ran for mayor of Cincinnati, Ohio, in 2005?

A. Nick Lachey

B. Drew Lachey

C. Jeff Timmons

D. Justin Jeffre

22. True or False: Drew Lachey opened Lachey Arts performing arts day camp in Ohio with his wife Lea.

23. What festival did 98 Degrees reunite for in 2012, which eventually led to them reuniting fully and recording new music?

A. Coachella

B. Music Midtown

C. Mixtape

D. Bonnaroo

24. What was the name of 98 Degrees' comeback single in 2013?

A. "Love Yourself"

B. "Microphone"

C. "The Package"

D. "Girls Night Out"

25. What was the name of the new single that 98 Degrees released in 2021?

A. "What Do You Want from Me?"

B. "Who Do You Love?"

C. "Where Do You Wanna Go?"

D. "Where Do We Go from Here?"

Answers: 1. A; 2. C; 3. D; 4. B; 5. A; 6. D; 7. B; 8. A; 9. B; 10. D; 11. C; 12. B; 13. A; 14. False; 15. A; 16. C; 17. B; 18. C; 19. A; 20. B; 21. D; 22. True; 23. C; 24. B; 25. C

BONUS
3DEEP

A lot of American boy band fans have never heard of 3Deep, but those in Canada, Asia, and Europe sure have. The band, however, only had one Canadian member—the other two members were from the United States. Their debut album featured a mix of upbeat pop tracks and soulful R&B ballads, though their only Top 10 hit in Canada was "Into You." While 3Deep's time together was relatively short-lived, their music from the late '90s remains a nostalgic memory for fans of the era.

1. What soap opera did both Joshua Morrow and Eddie Cibrian star in from 1994 to 1996? (Here's a hint: Joshua is still a cast member today.)

A. *Days of Our Lives*

B. *The Young and the Restless*

C. *General Hospital*

D. *The Bold and the Beautiful*

2. What was the name of 3Deep's debut album, which was released in 1999?

A. *Yes. No. Maybe*

B. *Can't Get Over You*

C. *Yes Yes Yes . . . No No No*

D. *Into You*

3. Which Backstreet Boy worked with 3Deep on their second album?

A. Nick Carter

B. Kevin Richardson

C. Brian Littrell

D. Howie Dorough

4. True or False: CJ Huyer was the only member of 3Deep that wasn't an actor.

5. Eddie Cibrian is now married to which country singer?

A. Carrie Underwood

B. LeAnn Rimes

C. Miranda Lambert

D. Lee Ann Womack

Answers: 1. B; 2. C; 3. D; 4. True; 5. B

1980s & 1990s

hanson

Hanson is made up of three brothers who burst onto the scene in 1997, even though they had been making music since 1992. They hit pop star celebrity status and graced the cover of magazines from *Tiger Beat* to *Bop*. But unlike a lot of the other boy groups that were in the magazines at the time, the Hanson brothers were musicians as well as performers. The group was praised for their abilities, including writing their own songs and playing various instruments. They drew influences from classic rock and soul, and their sound was often characterized by catchy melodies and attractive harmonies.

Hanson left an indelible mark on the music industry, and they have consistently demonstrated resilience, musical versatility, and a deep connection with their fan base. Known for their harmonious vocals and impressive musicianship, Hanson has continued to make music and tour, showcasing their enduring talent.

hanson

1. Where are the Hanson brothers originally from?

A. Atlanta, Georgia

B. Tulsa, Oklahoma

C. Birmingham, Alabama

D. Charleston, South Carolina

2. What name did Hanson go by originally?

A. Hanson Brothers

B. Brothers Hanson

C. 3X Hanson

D. The Hansons

3. Who is the oldest Hanson brother?

A. Taylor

B. Zac

C. Trevor

D. Isaac

4. How many Hanson siblings are there?

A. 8

B. 7

C. 4

D. 10

5. How old was Zac when they shot the music video for "MMMBop?"

A. 10

B. 11

C. 12

D. 13

6. What are the names of the two albums Hanson recorded in Tulsa before being signed to a major label?

A. *MMMBop and Hanson*

B. *Boomerang and Hanson*

C. *Hanson and Jealous*

D. *Boomerang and MMMBop*

7. What musical festival did Hanson play in 1994, which led them to signing with their first professional manager?

A. Coachella

B. Music Midtown

C. South by Southwest

D. Bonnaroo

8. What label did Hanson sign with to release their first album, *Middle of Nowhere*?

A. Mercury

B. Arista

C. Jive

D. Decca

9. What day was declared "Hanson Day" in their hometown?

A. April 1

B. May 6

C. July 12

D. October 19

10. In how many countries did "MMMBop" earn the No. 1 spot on local music charts?

A. 5

B. 8

C. 12

D. 19

11. *Middle of Nowhere* did not go to No. 1 in which country?

A. United Kingdom

B. Australia

C. United States

D. Germany

12. What song was not a single on *Middle of Nowhere*?

A. "Where's The Love"

B. "Speechless"

C. "I Will Come To You"

D. "Weird"

13. True or False: Hanson wrote every song on *Middle of Nowhere*.

14. What is the title of Hanson's second label release?

A. *Boomerang*

B. *Strong Enough to Break*

C. *This Time Around*

D. *Underneath*

15. Where was their Christmas album, *Snowed In*, recorded?

A. Tulsa, Oklahoma

B. London, England

C. New York, New York

D. Los Angeles, California

16. After leaving their major record label, Hanson created their own. What is it called?

A. 3CG Records

B. Hanson Records

C. 3H3 Records

D. Hanson, Inc.

17. Hanson created a documentary about what they went through when leaving their major label. What was the name of the documentary?

A. *MMMWhat?*

B. *Underneath*

C. *Strong Enough to Break*

D. *The Walk*

18. Where did Taylor get married?

A. Atlanta, Georgia

B. Pine Mountain, Georgia

C. Jekyll Island, Georgia

D. Macon, Georgia

19. On the tenth anniversary of Hanson Day, the band rerecorded which of their albums at a bar in their hometown?

A. *Snowed In*

B. *Middle of Nowhere*

C. *Underneath*

D. *The Walk*

20. In 2013, Hanson launched their own beer. What is it called?

A. MMMHops

B. Hanson Brothers Beer

C. BeerBop

D. Hanson Beer

21. Taylor is part of another band, which features members of the Smashing Pumpkins, Fountains of Wayne, and Cheap Trick. What is the name of the band?

A. Fast Cars & Freedom

B. Little Birds

C. Tinted Windows

D. The Band

22. In which pop star's video did Hanson make a special appearance?

A. Taylor Swift, "End Game"

B. Katy Perry, "Last Friday Night (T.G.I.F.)"

C. Pink, "So What?"

D. Britney Spears, "Boys"

23. What does the group do before every show?

A. Walk a mile barefoot

B. Have a boxing match

C. Watch their "MMMBop" music video

D. Play an acoustic show for their fan club

24. What is the name of Hanson's podcast?

A. *Deep Thoughts with Hanson*

B. *HMMRevelations*

C. *HANSON Time*

D. *It's About Time*

25. What costume did Hanson appear in on Season 5 of The Masked Singer?

A. Russian dolls

B. Teddy bears

C. Beer bottles

D. Ants

Answers: 1. B; 2. A; 3. D; 4. B; 5. B; 6. D; 7. C; 8. A; 9. B; 10. C; 11. C; 12. B; 13. True; 14. C; 15. C; 16. A; 17. C; 18. B; 19. B; 20. A; 21. C; 22. B; 23. A; 24. C; 25. A

BONUS
BBMAK

Some wouldn't consider BBMak, a British band consisting of three members, a boy band, because they're known for playing instruments and do not dance like the boy bands of their era. But their song "Back Here" was a staple on *TRL* after being featured on the Disney Channel's In Concert series, much like NSYNC. They also sold over three million albums between 1999 and 2003 and released two albums. After going their separate ways in 2003, the band came back together in 2018 to record a new album and toured the United States before the COVID-19 pandemic.

1. BBMak's debut single, "Back Here," reached the Top 10 in which country?

A. United Kingdom

B. United States

C. Australia

D. Brazil

2. Who gave the group its name?

A. Mark Barry

B. Christian Burns

C. Stephen McNally

D. Kevin Richardson

3. What instrument do two of the three members play onstage during shows?

A. Guitar

B. Keyboard

C. Drums

D. Tambourine

4. "Back Here" was cowritten by all the members of BBMak and a member of what band?

A. Rolling Stones

B. Hall and Oates

C. The Cure

D. AC/DC

5. When did BBMak release their third studio album?

A. 1999

B. 2001

C. 2008

D. 2019

Answers: 1. A; 2. C; 3. A; 4. C; 5. D

B2K was formed by choreographer Dave Scott and A&R executive Keisha Gamble and was introduced to the world by powerhouse producer Jermaine Dupri. Made up of members Omarion, J-Boog, Raz-B, and Lil' Fizz, B2K not only contributed to the R&B and hip-hop landscape but also left a positive mark on the hearts of their dedicated fan base, made up of mostly teenage girls. B2K's musical versatility meant that a number of their songs became anthems of the early 2000s R&B and hip-hop scene. The group became a regular fixture on MTV's *TRL* with their slick harmonies and dance moves.

While B2K's tenure as a group was short-lived, they left positive influences on the music scene and entertainment industry with several members taking the leap to solo and acting careers.

1. **What does B2K stand for?**

A. Back to Kansas

B. Boys of the New Millennium

C. Boys 2000

D. Band to Kings

2. **Who did B2K open for in 2001 before releasing their first single?**

A. Faith Evans

B. Backstreet Boys

C. NSYNC

D. Lil' Bow Wow

3. **Who is the youngest member of B2K?**

A. Lil' Fizz

B. Raz-B

C. Omarion

D. J-Boog

4. **True or False:** Omarion's real first name is Omari.

5. **Which member of B2K had previously appeared in TV commercials for McDonalds?**

A. Lil' Fizz

B. Omarion

C. J-Boog

D. Raz-B

6. **Where is Raz-B from originally?**

A. Louisville, Kentucky

B. Atlanta, Georgia

C. Cleveland, Ohio

D. Tampa, Florida

7. **Who was the first member of B2K?**

A. J-Boog

B. Omarion

C. Raz-B

D. Lil' Fizz

B2K

8. Who produced their first single, "Uh Huh"?

A. Jermaine Dupri

B. Tricky Stewart

C. Sean "Puffy" Combs

D. Missy Elliott

9. Which *Glee* cast member was in the B2K video for "Why I Love You"?

A. Melissa Benoist

B. Dianna Agron

C. Jenna Ushkowitz

D. Naya Rivera

10. Which star of *The Vampire Diaries* also appears in the "Why I Love You" music video?

A. Kat Graham

B. Nina Dobrev

C. Ian Somerhalder

D. Sara Canning

11. What is the name of B2K's Christmas album?

A. *Yo, Santa!*

B. *Santa, Here We Are*

C. *Santa Hooked Me Up*

D. *Rain and Snow*

12. True or False: "Bump, Bump, Bump" became the group's first No. 1 song on the *Billboard* Hot 100 chart.

13. Which R&B star cowrote "Bump, Bump, Bump"?

A. Jermaine Dupri
B. Wanya Morris
C. R. Kelly
D. Brian McKnight

14. Who played the "Godfather" in the music video for "Girlfriend"?

A. Chris Rock
B. Chris Tucker
C. Will Smith
D. The Rock

15. What award did B2K win at the 2003 Nickelodeon Kids' Choice Awards?

A. Favorite Song
B. Favorite Music Video
C. Favorite Group
D. Favorite Album

16. In which 2004 movie did B2K appear?

A. *Mean Girls*
B. *Sleepover*
C. *You Got Served*
D. *EuroTrip*

17. Which award has the group *not* been nominated for?

A. Video of the Year at the BET Awards

B. American Music Award for Favorite Hip-Hop/R&B New Artist

C. Top New Artist at the *Billboard* Music Awards

D. Best Group Video at the VMAs

18. What did B2K cite as the reason for breaking up in 2004?

A. Internal disagreements

B. Unhappiness

C. Fighting over the same woman

D. Disputes over musical direction

19. What was the name of Omarion's first solo album?

A. *O*

B. *Omarion*

C. *Face Off*

D. *Ollusion*

20. True or False: Omarion won a Grammy for Best Contemporary R&B Album at the 48th Annual Grammy Awards.

21. What reality series featured both Lil' Fizz and Omarion?

A. *Keeping Up with the Kardashians*

B. *The Real Housewives of Orange County*

C. *Love & Hip Hop*

D. *The Bachelor*

22. When did B2K announce they were reuniting?

A. December 25, 2017

B. December 31, 2018

C. December 31, 2019

D. December 22, 2018

23. What is the name of the tour that B2K launched that featured Mario, Ying Yang Twins, Pretty Ricky, and more?

A. B2K is B2Back

B. The Millennium Tour

C. B2K and Friends

D. Into the Millennium

24. Which member of B2K caused a lot of drama during their 2019 reunion tour, including being arrested in Minneapolis?

A. Raz-B

B. Omarion

C. J-Boog

D. Lil' Fizz

25. In 2022, which member of B2K called the other members "glorified backup dancers"?

A. J-Boog

B. Lil' Fizz

C. Omarion

D. Raz-B

Answers: 1. B; 2. D; 3. A; 4. True; 5. B; 6. C; 7. A; 8. B; 9. D; 10. A; 11. C; 12. True; 13. C; 14. C; 15. C; 16. C; 17. C; 18. A; 19. A; 20. False; 21. C; 22. B; 23. B; 24. A; 25. C

BONUS
SOULDECISION

Another Canadian pop band, soulDecision, hailed from Vancouver, British Columbia, and formed in 1993, but they didn't hit it big outside Canada until 2000, when the boy band craze was in full effect. Led by singer Trevor Guthrie, the group—which never claimed to be a boy band—fit right into the trend, especially with Guthrie's blond hair and luscious voice. The group opened for the likes of Christina Aguilera and NSYNC before disbanding in 2005.

1. What was soulDecision's original name?

A. Guthrie's Group

B. Indecision

C. Soul for Real

D. Cand Hold Us

2. SoulDecision's best performing song was what?

A. "Gravity"

B. "Feelin' You"

C. "Faded"

D. "Stay"

3. SoulDecision reached No. 1 on MTV's *TRL* with which song?

A. "Ooh It's Kinda Crazy"

B. "Let's Do It Better"

C. "Only in My Mind"

D. "No One Does It Better"

4. Which member of soulDecision attempted a solo career after they broke up?

A. David Bowman

B. Terepai Richmond

C. Trevor Guthrie

D. Simon Danson

5. "Faded" peaked at what number on the *Billboard* Hot 100?

A. 10

B. 15

C. 22

D. 27

Answers: 1. B; 2. C; 3. A; 4. C; 5. C

2000s

2000s

O-TOWN

Once Backstreet Boys and NSYNC left Lou Pearlman, he had to find the next big thing. After coming up with the idea for a television show to document how you create a boy band, Pearlman created *Making the Band* for ABC, to find the next big boy band. Thousands of young men from around the country—and the world—came to Orlando, Florida, to audition. Several of those hopefuls were moved into a house for "boy band boot camp."

Eventually, five young men were chosen to become Pearlman's newest boy band, O-Town, named for Orlando, the boy band capital of the world. Having gotten their start on TV, O-Town made a distinct mark on the next boy band phase in the new millennium and on the music industry as a whole. While they may not have reached the iconic status of some of their contemporaries, O-Town remains an important part of the pop music landscape and holds a special place in the hearts of their fans.

2000s

O-TOWN

1. When did *Making the Band* premiere on ABC?

A. 2002

B. 2005

C. 1999

D. 2000

2. Who was the first member of O-Town to be introduced on *Making the Band*?

A. Dan Miller

B. Ashley Parker Angel

C. Trevor Penick

D. Jacob Underwood

3. Where did Ashley Parker Angel audition for *Making the Band*?

A. Los Angeles

B. Dallas

C. Atlanta

D. Las Vegas

4. Who is the oldest member of O-Town?

A. Ashley Parker Angel

B. Erik-Michael Estrada

C. Dan Miller

D. Trevor Penick

5. Who was an original member of O-Town, before leaving and then being replaced by Dan Miller?

A. Steve Parker

B. Ikaika Kahoano

C. Koa Akamu

D. Kaimana Stephens

6. O-Town was signed to J Records by Clive Davis. Who was another of his famous clients?

A. Mariah Carey

B. Reba McEntire

C. Whitney Houston

D. Christina Aguilera

7. What was the name of O-Town's first single?

A. "All or Nothing"

B. "Liquid Dreams"

C. "Sexiest Woman Alive"

D. "Every Six Seconds"

8. Who is not mentioned in O-Town's debut single?

A. Destiny's Child

B. Madonna

C. Britney Spears

D. Halle Berry

9. What boy band was originally supposed to record "All or Nothing"?

A. Backstreet Boys

B. NSYNC

C. Take That

D. Westlife

10. "All or Nothing" went to No. 1 on the US Mainstream Top 40 *Billboard* chart, but went to what number on the US *Billboard* Hot 100?

A. 5

B. 10

C. 3

D. 2

11. When was O-Town's self-titled debut album released?

A. January 1, 2001

B. January 23, 2001

C. February 15, 2001

D. March 1, 2001

12. Overall, how many albums has O-Town sold?

A. 1 million

B. 3 million

C. 5 million

D. 8 million

13. Who did O-Town open up for in 2001?

A. Backstreet Boys

B. Whitney Houston

C. Britney Spears

D. Jessica Simpson

14. What was the name of O-Town's second album?

A. *Second Chances*

B. *O2*

C. *Orlando Calling*

D. *CO2*

15. "We Fit Together" was featured on what movie soundtrack?

A. *Legally Blonde*

B. *Rockstar*

C. *Dr. Doolittle 2*

D. *Donnie Darko*

16. After disbanding, who was the first member of O-Town to release an album?

A. Jacob Underwood

B. Ashley Parker Angel

C. Trevor Penick

D. Dan Miller

17. What was the name of Jacob Underwood's band?

A. Jacob's Loc

B. Jacob's Ladder

C. Fusion

D. Empty Space

18. What was the name of Ashley Parker Angel's reality TV show on MTV?

A. *After O-Town*

B. *Back to Reality*

C. *There and Back*

D. *The Future*

19. Which member of O-Town went back to school to get a degree in graphic design?

A. Dan MIller

B. Jacob Underwood

C. Trevor Penick

D. Erik-Michael Estada

20. Which member of O-Town declined to return when the band decided to get back together in 2013?

A. Dan Miller

B. Trevor Penick

C. Jacob Underwood

D. Ashley Parker Angel

21. What was the name of the group's third album, released in 2014?

A. *O3*

B. *Lines and Circles*

C. *Soundtrack to Your Life*

D. *O-Town Part 2*

22. Which well-known singer and producer worked with O-Town on their reunion album?

A. Shawn Mendes

B. Mikky Ekko

C. Ryan Tedder

D. Zedd

23. Which group did O-Town tour with in 2016?

A. 98 Degrees

B. Backstreet Boys

C. NSYNC

D. Big Time Rush

24. True or False: Universal Music Group told O-Town their name was too much like "Motown" when the group filed to trademark their band's name.

25. In 2018, O-Town, along with Ryan Cabrera and Tyler Hilton, started a tour that is still active today. What is the name of the tour?

A. Pop Tarts

B. 2000 Boys

C. Pop 2000

D. O-Town and Friends

Answers: 1. D; 2. C; 3. D; 4. B; 5. B; 6. C; 7. B; 8. C; 9. D; 10. C; 11. B; 12. B; 13. C; 14. B; 15. C; 16. B; 17. A; 18. C; 19. A; 20. D; 21. B; 22. C; 23. A; 24. True; 25. C

BONUS
2GETHER

As the Backstreet Boys and NSYNC rocked the charts, MTV decided to have a little fun of their own. They created a fictional boy band—with very real songs—for a movie. Both the movie and its satirical group were called 2Gether. The movie, directed by Nigel Dick, who was famous for directing several classic Backstreet Boys music videos, premiered on February 21, 2000, on MTV. The company was surprised when the band's music actually hit the *Billboard* charts.

1. **What was the name of 2Gether's most popular song in the movie?**

A. "Rub One Out"

B. "The Hardest Part of Breaking Up"

C. "U + Me = Us (Calculus)"

D. "Say It (Don't Spray It)"

2. **What was the name of 2Gether's rival in the movie?**

A. Whoa!

B. Abracadabra

C. 4Eva

D. Hot 4 Moms

3. Which actor passed away while filming the group's TV show, *2Gether: The Series*?

A. Evan Farmer (Jerry)

B. Noah Bastian (Chad)

C. Alex Solowitz (Mickey)

D. Michael Cuccione (Q.T.)

4. How many albums did 2Gether release?

A. 1

B. 2

C. 3

D. 4

5. Which Backstreet Boy wrote the single "Every Minute, Every Hour" for 2Gether?

A. Brian Littrell

B. Kevin Richardson

C. Nick Carter

D. Howie Dorough

Answers: 1. C; 2. A; 3. D; 4. B; 5. D

I ♥
JB
I ♥
JB
I ♥
JB

2000s

JONAS BROTHERS

What stands out about the Jonas Brothers is their enduring commitment to creating catchy, heartfelt, and relatable music. They seamlessly blend elements of pop, rock, and R&B, crafting songs that not only get stuck in your head but also touch your heart. Much like Hanson, they weren't the typical boy band. They played their own instruments and were the architects of anthems that became the soundtrack to the lives of millions of millennial teenagers around the world.

From their early days on the Disney Channel to their mature and more personal work in later years, the Jonas Brothers have shown growth and versatility in their artistry. Their contribution to the music industry and their ability to connect with people through their music and personalities make them a cherished and enduring part of pop culture.

JONAS BROTHERS

1. Where are the Jonas Brothers from?

A. Dallas, Texas

B. Wyckoff, New Jersey

C. Charlotte, North Carolina

D. Trenton, New Jersey

2. What name did the brothers think about using before they decided on Jonas Brothers?

A. The Brothers Jonas

B. Jonas

C. Sons of Jonas

D. KJN

3. True or False: Nick Jonas was originally signed to Columbia Records as a solo act, then he introduced his brothers and a song they wrote called "Please Be Mine."

4. Who is the oldest Jonas Brother?

A. Nick Jonas

B. Joe Jonas

C. Frankie Jonas

D. Kevin Jonas

5. Nick was in commercials for which restaurant chain when he was a kid?

A. Applebee's

B. Longhorn

C. Chuck E. Cheese

D. McDonald's

6. Who did the Jonas Brothers *not* open for while recording their debut album?

A. Kelly Clarkson

B. Backstreet Boys

C. Destiny's Child

D. Jesse McCartney

7. What was the name of the Jonas Brothers' first album?

A. *Year 3000*

B. *Hold On*

C. *Please Be Mine*

D. *It's About Time*

8. The band was dropped by Columbia Records in 2007 and was later signed by Disney-owned Hollywood Records. The label quickly rereleased a previous single by the Jonas Brothers. What was the single?

A. "Hold On"

B. "Year 3000"

C. "Mandy"

D. "Please Be Mine"

9. Where did Kevin meet his future wife, Danielle?

A. New York City

B. Miami

C. Los Angeles

D. The Bahamas

10. The Jonas Brothers appeared in a popular TV show, in an episode called "Me and Mr. Jonas and Mr. Jonas and Mr. Jonas." What was the show?

A. *Grey's Anatomy*

B. *Hannah Montana*

C. *Gossip Girl*

D. *Private Practice*

11. At what position did their album *Jonas Brothers* debut on the *Billboard* charts?

A. No. 1

B. No. 5

C. No. 10

D. No. 8

12. What was the name of the short series the Jonas Brothers starred in on the Disney Channel while on their Look Me in the Eyes Tour?

A. *Jonas Brothers: Living the Dream*

B. *On Tour: Jonas Brothers*

C. *Jonas Brothers: On Tour*

D. *Behind the Scenes: Jonas Brothers*

13. The Jonas Brothers made their film debut in which movie?

A. *Hannah Montana: The Movie*

B. *Sleepover*

C. *What Happens in Vegas*

D. *Camp Rock*

14. Which fellow artists were featured in the concert film *Jonas Brothers: The 3D Concert Experience*?

A. Taylor Swift and Selena Gomez

B. Selena Gomez and Demi Lovato

C. Miley Cyrus and Taylor Swift

D. Taylor Swift and Demi Lovato

15. True or False: The Jonas Brothers were the youngest band to ever be featured on *Rolling Stone's* cover.

16. What life event happened to Nick on the same day the group shot the album cover for *Lines, Vines, and Trying Times*?

A. He graduated from high school
B. He got his driver's license
C. He had his first kiss
D. He went to prom

17. What is the name of Joe Jonas's solo album, released in 2011?

A. *Fastlife*
B. *Kleptomaniac*
C. *Just in Love*
D. *Sorry*

18. True or False: "First Time" was the first single released from *V*, the Jonas Brothers' album that was ultimately never released.

19. Who was the first Jonas Brother to become a dad?

A. Joe Jonas
B. Kevin Jonas
C. Frankie Jonas
D. Nick Jonas

20. Nick Jonas dabbled in acting after the Jonas Brothers broke up. In what TV show did he play a character named Boone Clemens?

A. *American Horror Story*

B. *Hawaii 5-0*

C. *Scream Queens*

D. *Grey's Anatomy*

21. When did the Jonas Brothers announce their comeback?

A. March 1, 2020

B. February 28, 2019

C. February 2, 2018

D. March 5, 2019

22. "Sucker," the first single from the Jonas Brothers' comeback album *Happiness Begins*, became the first No. 1 on the *Billboard* Hot 100 chart by a boy band since which song?

A. Backstreet Boys' "I Want It That Way"

B. B2K's "Bump, Bump, Bump"

C. One Direction's "What Makes You Beautiful"

D. NSYNC's "Bye Bye Bye"

23. What is the name of the documentary the Jonas Brothers released on Amazon Prime?

A. *Happiness Begins Again*

B. *Chasing Happiness*

C. *Runaway*

D. *Brothers Forever*

24. When did the Jonas Brothers receive their star on the Hollywood Walk of Fame?

A. January 30, 2023

B. January 10, 2023

C. February 9, 2023

D. March 10, 2022

25. *The Album* debuted at No. 3 on the *Billboard* 200 chart in 2023. How many albums have the Jonas Brothers had debut in the Top 10?

A. 10

B. 8

C. 7

D. 5

Answers: 1. B; 2. C; 3. True; 4. D; 5. C; 6. C; 7. D; 8. B; 9. D; 10. B; 11. B; 12. A; 13. D; 14. D; 15. True; 16. B; 17. A; 18. False; 19. B; 20. C; 21. B; 22. B; 23. B; 24. A; 25. D

BONUS
DREAM STREET

Dream Street, like other boy bands, was put together by music producers and consisted of boys who had been on Broadway and had professional backgrounds in the acting world. Unlike the other boy bands of the time, though, they were all actually *boys*, ranging in age from eleven to fourteen. After the group disbanded in 2002, band member Jesse McCartney embarked on a successful solo and songwriting career. The group got back together in 2023, after the tragic death of one of their bandmates.

1. What was Dream Street's original name?

A. Dreamstreet
B. Boy Wonder
C. Bach Porch Boys
D. A Boy's World

2. On which movie soundtrack did Dream Street's song "They Don't Understand" appear?

A. *What a Girl Wants*
B. *13 Going on 30*
C. *Pokemon 2000*
D. *Mean Girls*

3. The final Dream Street release was the soundtrack to *The Biggest Fan*, which was a movie starring which Dream Street member?

A. Jesse McCartney

B. Greg Rapaso

C. Frankie Galasso

D. Chris Trousdale

4. What song did Jesse McCartney write in 2007 that went No. 1 in thirty-five countries?

A. "Because of You" by Neo

B. "Umbrella" by Rihanna

C. "Burning Love" by Leona Lewis

D. "Makes Me Wonder" by Maroon 5

5. After Chris Trousdale's death in 2020, the group got together to virtually perform which Dream Street song?

A. "It Happens Every Time"

B. "I Say Yeah"

C. "With All My Heart"

Answers: 1. B; 2. C; 3. D; 4. C; 5. A

2000s

BIG TIME RUSH

Like the Monkees before them, Big Time Rush was initially put together for a television show (aptly titled *Big Time Rush*) and then eventually became a real band, recording and releasing singles long after the show ended. In fact, one of the show's executive producers said that the Monkees were his inspiration for the group.

While the TV show consisted of four hockey players from Minnesota, the band consisted entirely of actors, each with soap opera, drama, sitcom, or music backgrounds. The group's journey, which started from a scripted television series and found them becoming a real-life pop sensation, is a noteworthy and interesting facet of boy band history. After breaking up in 2014, the group came back together in 2021 to release new music and go on several successful tours. They no longer have to play fictional versions of themselves and can be the real band they were always meant to be.

2000s

BIG TIME RUSH

1. What network did *Big Time Rush* appear on?

A. Disney Channel

B. ABC

C. Nickelodeon

D. Lifetime

2. Who were the first two members of *Big Time Rush* to be cast?

A. Carlos Pena Jr. and Kendall Schmidt

B. James Maslow and Logan Henderson

C. Logan Henderson and Carlos Pena Jr.

D. Kendall Schmidt and James Maslow

3. At which school had Carlos Pena Jr. started before auditioning for the show?

A. Boston Conservatory

B. Boston College

C. Harvard

D. New York University

4. Which soap opera did Kendall Schmidt have a reoccurring role on prior to joining *Big Time Rush*?

A. *The Young and the Restless*

B. *As the World Turns*

C. *General Hospital*

D. *Days of Our Lives*

5. What was the title of the hour-long pilot episode of *Big Time Rush*?

A. "Big Time Show"

B. "Big Time Audition"

C. "Big Time Decision"

D. "Big Time Beginning"

6. What Nickelodeon show did James Maslow previously have a role on?

A. *iCarly*

B. *Drake & Josh*

C. *Victorious*

D. *Zoey 101*

7. What record label did the group initially sign with, at the same time as they signed their TV contracts?

A. Hollywood Records

B. Arista Records

C. Nick Records

D. Jive Records

8. What was the name of Big Time Rush's first song, released on November 20, 2009? (It would go on to be the show's theme song.)

A. "Til I Forget About You"

B. "Big Time Rush"

C. "Boyfriend"

D. "Worldwide"

9. Which of the band's songs was the first to chart on the *Billboard* Hot 100?

A. "Any Kind of Guy"

B. "Til I Forget About You"

C. "Famous"

D. "Halfway There"

10. What was the name of the group's first album, which debuted at No. 3 on the *Billboard* 200 chart?

A. *BTR*

B. *Big Time Rush*

C. *Boyfriend*

D. *Famous*

11. Which rapper performed on the group's song "Boyfriend"?

A. Eminem

B. Dr. Dre

C. Snoop Dogg

D. 50 Cent

12. Which song earned a gold certification for shipping over 500,000 physical copies in the United States?

A. "City Is Ours"

B. "Til I Forget About You"

C. "Big Night"

D. "Boyfriend"

13. What was James Maslow's last name on the show?

A. Knight

B. Diamond

C. Maslow

D. Wainwright

14. True or False: The band's first album went platinum, selling over a million copies.

15. What was the name of Big Time Rush's second album?

A. *Elevate*

B. *Music*

C. *Windows Down*

D. *Worldwide*

16. Who opened for Big Time Rush on ten dates of their Better with U tour?

A. Ariana Grande

B. Taylor Swift

C. One Direction

D. The Wanted

17. What was the name of the first episode of Season 4 of *Big Time Rush*, which discussed the history of boy bands and Big Time Rush's new rival, One Direction?

A. "Big Time Rival"

B. "Big Time Invasion"

C. "Big Time Surprise"

D. "Big Time Trust Issue"

18. Which award did Big Time Rush win at the 2014 World Music Awards?

A. Best Pop Act

B. Best-Selling American Group

C. Best Live Act

D. Best Album (24/Seven)

19. When did the last episode of *Big Time Rush* air?

A. November 10, 2012

B. July 25, 2013

C. July 10, 2013

D. November 15, 2013

20. True or False: When Carlos married actress Alexa Vega, they took the last name PenaVega, merging their two last names.

21. Which two members of *Big Time Rush* have competed on *Dancing with the Stars*?

A. Carlos PenaVega and James Maslow

B. Carlos PenaVega and Logan Henderson

C. Logan Henderson and James Maslow

D. Kendall Schmidt and Carlos PenaVega

22. James Maslow starred in what Lifetime movie based on a book from the Flowers in the Attic series?

A. *Petals in the Wind*

B. *Garden of Shadows*

C. *Seeds of Yesterday*

D. *If There Be Thorns*

23. Which song did Big Time Rush perform acoustically and virtually during the COVID-19 pandemic, before their eventual reunion announcement?

A. "Like Nobody's Around"

B. "Worldwide"

C. "Honey"

D. "Call It Like I See it"

24. When did Big Time Rush announce their reunion?

A. June 19, 2021

B. July 19, 2021

C. July 20, 2021

D. July 21, 2022

25. What was the name of the group's 2023 tour?

A. Worldwide

B. Big Time Again

C. Can't Get Enough

D. Boyfriends on the Road

Answers: 1. C; 2. B; 3. A; 4. C; 5. B; 6. A; 7. C; 8. B; 9. D; 10. A; 11. C; 12. D; 13. B; 14. True; 15. A; 16. C; 17. B; 18. C; 19. B; 20. True; 21. A; 22. C; 23. B; 24. B; 25. C

BONUS
CNCO

Like One Direction, CNCO came together after auditioning for a reality show. CNCO tried out for the first season of *La Banda*, a Univision singing competition that was created by none other than Simon Cowell and Ricky Martin (a former Menudo member). After competing on the show in 2015, the band was formed on the last episode, and the rest is history. The group, which is still going strong, continues to have success, especially in the Latin market.

1. What does the name CNCO refer to?

A. The band members' initials
B. The number five in Spanish
C. The members' hometowns
D. The school they went to

2. What did the band receive after winning *La Banda*?

A. New cars
B. A management deal
C. A five-year recording contract
D. A five-album deal

3. Where did CNCO hold their first concert?

A. Hard Rock Café in Orlando

B. Planet Hollywood in Miami

C. The Fillmore at Miami Beach

D. On the internet

4. What was the name of their debut single?

A. "Tan Fácil"

B. "Devuélveme Mi Corazón"

C. "Reggaetón Lento (Bailemos)"

D. "Todo Cambió"

5. Which member left the band in 2021?

A. Richard Camacho

B. Joel Pimentel

C. Christopher Velez

D. Erick Brian Colón

Answers: 1. B; 2. C; 3. C; 4. A; 5. B

1D

2000s

ONE DIRECTION

Though they came after enormous acts like the Beatles, New Kids On The Block, Backstreet Boys, and the Jonas Brothers, One Direction was probably one of the biggest boy bands of all time (so far!). The group, which got their start on reality television, came together after judges moved contestants around to form a boy band.

From the group's rise and each member's eventual solo ventures, One Direction's story is one of success and artistic evolution. Their music and the memories they created continue to bring joy to fans, and their impact on the music industry remains profound, illustrating that it's possible for five talented performers to make sweet music together and then launch thriving solo careers. They have left a legacy in music that's about more than just chart-topping hits. Their legacy is one of community, and how fans can help drive bands to a bigger sphere of success than they ever dreamed.

ONE DIRECTION

1. On which reality competition show did One Direction form?

A. *American Idol*

B. *The X Factor*

C. *The Voice*

D. *America's Got Talent*

2. Who was the first member of One Direction chosen to join the band?

A. Liam Payne

B. Harry Styles

C. Louis Tomlinson

D. Niall Horan

3. Who was the last member to join?

A. Liam Payne

B. Zayn Malik

C. Harry Styles

D. Niall Horan

4. Who is the oldest member of One Direction?

A. Liam Payne

B. Zayn Malik

C. Harry Styles

D. Louis Tomlinson

5. Which song did Harry Styles sing during his solo audition?

A. "Gone" by NSYNC

B. "Always on My Mind" by Elvis Presley

C. "Isn't She Lovely" by Stevie Wonder

D. "Hey There Delilah" by Plain White T's

6. What was the first song One Direction performed as a group?

A. "Truly, Madly, Deeply" by Savage Garden

B. "I Want It That Way" by Backstreet Boys

C. "Lovebug" by Jonas Brothers

D. "Torn" by Natalie Imbruglia

7. What was the name of One Direction's first single, both internationally and in the United States?

A. "Up All Night"

B. "What Makes You Beautiful"

C. "Gotta Be You"

D. "One Thing"

8. On which show did One Direction make their US television debut?

A. *The Ellen DeGeneres Show*

B. *Good Morning America*

C. *The Today Show*

D. *The Tonight Show*

9. Which two members of One Direction have the same middle name (James)?

A. Harry and Liam

B. Liam and Zayn

C. Niall and Liam

D. Louis and Zayn

10. True or False: When their first album, *Up All Night*, debuted at No. 1 on the *Billboard* 200 chart, One Direction became the second British band to attain the honor.

11. Which award did One Direction *not* win at the 2012 MTV Video Music Awards?

A. Best New Artist

B. Best Pop Video

C. Most Share-Worthy Video

D. Best Video

12. Who wrote One Direction's "Take Me Home," the second single from their second album?

A. Ed Sheeran

B. Taylor Swift

C. Shawn Mendes

D. Joe Jonas

13. How many dates did One Direction sell out on their Take Me Home Tour at the O2 arena in London?

A. 4

B. 10

C. 6

D. 7

14. What was One Direction's highest charting single in the United States, reaching No. 2?

A. "Story of My Life"

B. "Midnight Memories"

C. "One Way or Another"

D. "Best Song Ever"

15. Who guest starred in the music video for "Steal My Girl"?

A. Taylor Swift

B. Danny DeVito

C. Cheryl Cole

D. Julia Roberts

16. With the release of *Four*, One Direction became the first band in history to do what?

A. Release two albums in the same year

B. Have their first four albums reach No. 1 on the *Billboard* 200

C. Sell three million copies in the first week

D. Write all the songs on all their albums

17. Which member of One Direction left the group abruptly in 2015?

A. Harry Styles

B. Zayn Malik

C. Louis Tomlinson

D. Liam Payne

18. In August 2015, One Direction announced what?

A. They were going on hiatus

B. They were adding a new fifth member

C. Harry Styles was leaving the band

D. They were going on tour

19. The song "Perfect," cowritten by Harry Styles and Louis Tomlinson, is said to be a response to what?

A. Zayn leaving the band

B. Taylor Swift writing songs about Harry

C. Their fans

D. Their dream girl

20. What was One Direction's last televised TV appearance before their hiatus?

A. *The X Factor*

B. *The Late, Late Show with James Corden*

C. *Dick Clark's New Year's Rockin' Eve*

D. *Good Morning America*

21. Who was the first One Direction member to release a solo single?

A. Harry Styles

B. Zayn Malik

C. Niall Horan

D. Liam Payne

22. True or False: "Slow Hands" by Niall Horan went to No. 1 on the US Adult Top 40, US Dance Club Songs, and US Mainstream Top 40 *Billboard* charts.

23. Which One Direction member had a child with former *X Factor* host Cheryl Cole?

A. Liam Payne

B. Harry Styles

C. Liam Tomlinson

D. Niall Horan

24. In 2020, Harry Styles became the first man to what?

A. Win Artist of the Year at the Grammys

B. Appear alone on the cover of *Vogue*

C. Wear a dress to the Academy Awards

D. Write a song that a female singer recorded that went to No. 1

25. How many American Music Awards did One Direction win while they were together?

A. 2

B. 7

C. 5

D. 10

Answers: 1. B; 2. D; 3. B; 4. D; 5. C; 6. D; 7. B; 8. C; 9. C; 10. False; 11. D; 12. A; 13. C; 14. D; 15. B; 16. B; 17. B; 18. A; 19. B; 20. C; 21. B; 22. True; 23. A; 24. B; 25. B

BONUS
THE WANTED

Around the same time that One Direction was getting started, there was another British-Irish boy band coming up. It took over nine months of auditions and behind-the-scenes work to finalize the group before they signed a record deal. While The Wanted had success in the United States, their career was a bit hotter in the United Kingdom. After breaking up in 2014, they announced they would reunite in 2021.

1. What was the name of The Wanted's debut single?

A. "Lose My Mind"

B. "All Time Low"

C. "Glad You Came"

D. "Warzone"

2. Which famous manager managed The Wanted?

A. Simon Cowell

B. Johnny Wright

C. Scooter Braun

D. Lou Pearlman

3. Who did The Wanted open for in Manchester, UK, in November 2011?

A. One Direction

B. Jonas Brothers

C. Ariana Grande

D. Britney Spears

4. True or False: "Glad You Came" peaked at No. 2 on the *Billboard* Hot 100 charts in the United States.

5. The Wanted released a song about one of the most popular female singers in the world. What was the name of the song?

A. "My Madonna"

B. "Walks Like Rihanna"

C. "Just Like Taylor"

D. "Classic Mariah"

Answers: 1. B; 2. C; 3. D; 4. False; 5. B

BTS

TS

BTS

BTS

BTS

2000s

BTS

BTS may have stormed onto the international music scene in 2017, but the group actually got their start seven years before that. They originally started as a hip-hop group in their home country of South Korea, at the behest of Big Hit Entertainment CEO Bang Si-hyuk (known as "Hitman" Bang). Bang wanted to create a group that could sell concert tickets because the music industry and record sales were on the decline. BTS became the biggest band to come out of South Korea and has played an instrumental part in bringing K-pop to the mainstream music industry.

2000s

BTS

1. Which was a potential name for the group before they landed on BTS?

A. STB

B. Popsicle

C. Big Kidz

D. Kidz of the Future

2. How many members does BTS have?

A. 5

B. 7

C. 9

D. 8

3. What does BTS stand for?

A. Behind The Scenes

B. Balance The Stardom

C. Bulletproof Boy Scouts

D. Brilliant Singers

4. How did RM learn English?

A. Watching *Friends*

B. Listening to Taylor Swift

C. Reading Harry Potter books

D. At school

5. Which member of BTS is afraid of microwaves?

A. Jin

B. Jungkook

C. RM

D. V

6. Who is the oldest member of BTS?

A. Jin

B. Suga

C. Jungkook

D. J-Hope

7. What was the name of BTS's first single?

A. "2 Cool 4 Skool"

B. "No More Dream"

C. "O!RUL8,2?"

D. "N.O."

8. What was the first BTS album to appear on *Billboard's* World Albums Chart?

A. *Dark & Wild*

B. *The Red Bullet*

C. *Skool Luv Affair*

D. *Open Your Eyes*

9. Where did BTS perform their first show in the United States?

A. Miami, Florida

B. New York, New York

C. Seattle, Washington

D. West Hollywood, California

10. What was the name of BTS's 2014 tour, with stops in Malaysia, Australia, North America, Latin America, and Japan?

A. Skool Luv Affair

B. Danger

C. Red Bullet Tour

D. The Show

11. True or False: BTS's album *The Most Beautiful Moment in Life Pt. 1* went to No. 2 on the US Independent Albums Chart.

12. BTS was the first group to win a *Billboard* Music Award in 2017. Which award was it?

A. Artist of the Year

B. Pop Song of the Year

C. Dance Hit of the Year

D. Top Social Artist

13. What BTS song was the first to crack the *Billboard* Hot 100, charting at No. 85?

A. "Love Yourself"

B. "DNA"

C. "Spring Day"

D. "Wings"

14. True or False: BTS's 2018 hit "Fake Love" went to No. 1 on *Billboard's* US Digital Song Sales chart and No. 10 on the US *Billboard* Hot 100 chart.

15. For which song did BTS collaborate with Steve Aoki?

A. "Waste It On Me"

B. "Fake Love"

C. "Idol"

D. "Burnin' Up"

16. The Hyundai Research Institute has determined that how many people visit South Korea every year because of BTS?

A. 1,000,000

B. 500,000

C. 800,000

D. 100,000

17. According to reports, BTS and what other artist were the only ones to sell at least 500,000 albums in 2020?

A. Harry Styles

B. Taylor Swift

C. Britney Spears

D. Jonas Brothers

18. BTS released their first English-language single on August 21, 2020. What was the name of the song?

A. "Stay Gold"

B. "Forever Mine"

C. "Dynamite"

D. "On"

19. What award did BTS *not* win at the 2020 MTV Music Video Awards?

A. Best Group Video

B. Best Video

C. Best Pop Video

D. Best K-Pop Video

20. True or False: When "Dynamite" was nominated for best Pop Duo/Group Performance at the 63rd Annual Grammy Awards in 2020, BTS was the second Korean act to be recognized by the Recording Academy.

21. Which BTS album did not occupy three spots on the Global Album Sales Chart of 2020?

A. Be (Deluxe Edition)

B. Map of the Soul: 7

C. Love Yourself: Speak Yourself

D. Map of the Soul: 7 – The Journey

22. With which band did BTS release the song "My Universe" in 2021?

A. Maroon 5

B. Coldplay

C. Backstreet Boys

D. Jonas Brothers

23. Which BTS member became the first Asian artist to perform at the FIFA World Cup in 2022?

A. Jin

B. V

C. RM

D. Jungkook

24. In May 2022, BTS became the first K-pop group to visit which landmark?

A. The Eiffel Tower

B. The White House

C. London Bridge

D. The Hollywood sign

25. Who was the first member of BTS to enlist in the Korean army?

A. J-Hope

B. V

C. Jin

D. Suga

Answers: 1. C; 2. B; 3. C (Their name in Korean is *Bangtan Sonyeondan*); 4. A; 5. B; 6. A; 7. B; 8. C; 9. D; 10. C; 11. False; 12. D; 13. B; 14. True; 15. A; 16. C; 17. B; 18. C; 19. B; 20. False; 21. C; 22. B; 23. D; 24. B; 25. C

BONUS
TOMORROW X TOGETHER

Put together by the same organization that gave the world BTS, Tomorrow X Together, also known as TXT, is relatively new to the music scene. The band started in 2019 and is still going strong. Unlike BTS, Tomorrow X Together quickly became a *Billboard* mainstay, having their first album debut at No. 140 on the *Billboard* 200 charts.

1. How many members of Tomorrow X Together are there?

A. 14

B. 5

C. 8

D. 7

2. Who is the oldest member of Tomorrow X Together?

A. Yeonjun

B. Beomgyu

C. Taehyn

D. Soobin

3. What was the name of Tomorrow X Together's EP?

A. *Part One: Stars*

B. *The Star Chapter: Outer Space*

C. *The Dream Chapter: Star*

D. *Bright Star*

4. True or False: *The Chaos Chapter: Freeze* debuted at No. 5 on the Billboard 200 chart in 2021, making it the group's highest-charting album in the United States.

5. In 2023, Tomorrow X Together released "Do It Like That" in the United States, a song featuring what group?

A. Backstreet Boys

B. Jonas Brothers

C. Big Time Rush

D. New Kids On The Block

Answers: 1. B; 2. A; 3. C; 4. True; 5. B

Just the FACTS
Best-Selling BOY BANDS

These are the Top 10 boy bands, based on millions of albums sold. Did your favorite make the list?

1.

BACKSTREET BOYS

(140+ million)

2.

THE JACKSON 5

(100 million)

3.

THE OSMONDS

(77 million)

4. **New Kids On The Block** (70 million)
5. **NSYNC** (70 million)
6. **One Direction** (70 million)
7. **Bay City Rollers** (70 million)
8. **Boyz II Men** (60 million)
9. **Take That** (45 million)
10. **Westlife** (45 million)

Longest-Running BOY BANDS

Your favorite band will always hold a special place in your heart, whether you fell in love with them five minutes ago or twenty-five years ago. These are some of the longest-running bands, based on the years they've been active. (Breakups and hiatuses don't count!)

1.

THE JACKSON 5

(37 years)

2.

BOYZ II MEN

(36 years)

3.

HANSON

(32 years)

4. **Backstreet Boys** (31 years)
5. **New Kids On The Block** (26 years)
6. **Take That** (24 years)
7. **The Osmonds** (22 years)
8. **98 Degrees** (18 years)
9. **Bay City Rollers** (15 years)
10. **Jonas Brothers** (13 years)

Which BOY BAND are you?

Sure, you're a fan, and maybe you've been following your favorite band for years. But do you think you have the right stuff to count yourself as one of the boys? After this quiz, you'll officially know to which band you truly belong.

1. What is most important to you when it comes to boy bands?

A. Hard work

B. Smooth harmonies

C. Killer dance moves

D. Having fun

2. If someone breaks up with you, what are you most likely to do?

A. Hang tough

B. Tell them to quit playing games with your heart

C. Tell them bye bye bye

D. Look back on all the midnight memories

3. What is your idea of a fun date?

A. A day game at Fenway

B. Heading anywhere that feels like home

C. A dirty pop party

D. A tour of London on a double-decker bus

4. Your best friend's significant other cheats on them. What do you say?

A. "What a dirty dawg . . ."

B. "Get another boyfriend!"

C. "It makes me ill."

D. "They are history."

5. How do you sign your holiday cards?

A. Have a funky, funky Christmas

B. Having a great Christmas in New York

C. Merry Christmas, Happy Holidays

D. It's Christmas Time!

6. If you were a boy band, what would your signature outfit be?

A. Ordinary, everyday clothes—but fashionable!

B. All white everything

C. Shiny leather jackets, no strings attached

D. Different styles for each member, but a cohesive look

7. Where would be the perfect place to shoot a video?

A. A graveyard

B. The middle of an empty field

C. An insane asylum

D. A fancy hotel

MOSTLY As: You've got the right stuff—You're NKOTB!

NEW KIDs ON THE BIOCK

You tell it like it is and keep things simple and old school with swag, because you're hangin' tough.

MOSTLY Bs: Quit playing games —You're Backstreet Boys!

BACKSTREET BOYS

You are all about the smooth harmonies, crisp outfits, and telling your friends what's what, because you want it that way.

MOSTLY Cs: Get ready to be a celebrity—You're NSYNC!

NSYNC

You have some of the best dance moves in boy band history and aren't afraid to tell people to go bye-bye-bye, to keep from driving yourself crazy.

MOSTLY Ds: You've got that one thing—you're One Direction!

ONE DIRECTION

You are all about having fun, singing sweet ballads, and creating memories. That's the story of your life!

Acknowledgments

I want to thank Katie and the Quarto Publishing crew, who have been wonderful to work with again. Working with you guys is so fun!

I want to thank my mom, who passed away in 2022, for exposing me to boy bands. She didn't care that she was buying her five-year-old daughter New Edition on cassette and, a few years later, Bel Biv DeVoe, only for me to get in trouble at school for playing "Do Me." She wasn't mad when I found her old Donny Osmond 45 of "Puppy Love," ran into the dining room, and slipped, almost tearing a ligament in my knee. She followed me to concerts all over the Southeast, almost running over Trevor from O-Town at an autograph signing, and to boat races to see Nick Carter. She supported my boy band habits until her dying day. The day before she died, Backstreet Boys released their Christmas CD and she joked to the nurse that she had a fever because Nick was so hot.

I want to thank my best friends who have gone to concerts with me even when they weren't crazy about the boy band. We may have met because of the Backstreet Boys, but they followed me to see New Kids On The Block, 98 Degrees, O-Town, Jonas Brothers, and more. Julia, Mara, and Lisa, I love you guys. To Julie, Emilia, and Melly, thank you for listening to me babble about the weird things I found out while writing this book.

I want to give a big shout-out to another one of my best friends, Amber, who helped me research some of the bands that I didn't know well.

To my oldest friend, my best friend, Amanda. From the day we met in ninth grade and talked about Garth Brooks to you finally meeting a Backstreet Boy in person, thank you for inspiring me to write Backstreet Boys fan fiction in 1998. It led me to where I am today.

To Joey Fatone—I finally have a book that you're in. Are you happy now?

To Joey McIntyre, Nick Carter, and Joe Jonas—you guys always keep a girl on her toes, especially you, Carter.

About the Author

Karah-Leigh Hancock has been a boy band fan pretty much since the day she was born. From loving New Edition and New Kids On The Block, to the Backstreet Boys and 98 Degrees, and then the Jonas Brothers and One Direction, she is a professional fangirl.

Her first concert was during New Kids On The Block's Summer Magic Tour when she was in the fourth grade and the first CD she bought with her own money was Boyz II Men's *II*. She is known for her intense knowledge of boy bands, especially Backstreet Boys, and released *Backstreet Boys 30th Anniversary Celebration* in April 2023 with her friend, Emilia Filogamo. She saw one of O-Town's very first concerts and was even on an episode of *Making the Band*. Plus, Joe Jonas looked her in the eyes.

Karah-Leigh is a former award-winning journalist and now works in marketing by day, but promotes her favorite group, Backstreet Boys, and her favorite boy, Nick Carter, by night. She currently lives in Atlanta with her cat, Madeleine (Maddie), who was named after a Backstreet Boys song.

When she's not promoting Backstreet Boys and Nick Carter, she's either at a concert, writing fiction (you can find her books online) or blogging on one of her websites, enjoying Marvel movies, watching the Atlanta Braves during baseball season, or keeping up with the latest news on Taylor Swift.

WEBSITES:

karahleigh.com

thefandemonium.com

bsbfangirls.com

Twitter/X: @KarahTheFangirl | @BSBFangirls | @the_fandemonium

Instagram: @karahleigh | @bsbfangirls | @_thefandemonium

First published in 2024 by Epic Ink,
an imprint of The Quarto Group,
142 West 36th Street, 4th Floor,
New York, NY 10018, USA
(212) 779-4972 www.Quarto.com

10 9 8 7 6 5 4 3 2 1

ISBN: 978-0-76039-014-6

Digital edition published in 2024
eISBN: 978-0-76039-015-3

Library of Congress Cataloging-in-Publication Data

Names: Hancock, Karah-Leigh, author.
Title: Boy bands ultimate trivia book : test your superfan status and relive the most iconic boy band moments / Karah-Leigh Hancock.
Description: New York : Epic Ink, 2024. | Summary: "Packed with hundreds of trivia questions, the Boy Bands Ultimate Trivia Book will test the expertise of every superfan"-- Provided by publisher.
Identifiers: LCCN 2024000110 (print) | LCCN 2024000111 (ebook) | ISBN 9780760390146 (paperback) | ISBN 9780760390153 (ebook)
Subjects: LCSH: Boy bands--Miscellanea. | Popular music--Miscellanea. | LCGFT: Trivia and miscellanea.
Classification: LCC ML3470 . H355 2024 (print) | LCC ML3470 (ebook) | DDC 782.42164092/2--dc23/eng/20240105
LC record available at https://lccn.loc.gov/2024000110
LC ebook record available at https://lccn.loc.gov/2024000111

Group Publisher: Rage Kindelsperger
Editorial Director: Lori Burke
Creative Director: Laura Drew
Managing Editor: Cara Donaldson
Editor: Katie McGuire
Cover Design: Scott Richardson
Interior Design: Maeve Bargman

Printed in China